BEST EVER
CLASSROOM
JOKES

BEST EVER
CLASSROOM
JOKES

Mike Haskins

PORTICO

$$\frac{x^2 - y^2}{\sqrt{z^2}} = 2\sqrt{\frac{(x^n - y^b)(3z + 2x - y^3)}{a^2 + b^2}}$$

CONTENTS

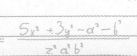

$$\frac{x^2 - y^2}{\sqrt{z^2}} = 2\sqrt{\frac{(x^n - y^b)(3z + 2x - y^3)}{a^2 + b^2}}$$

$$3\sqrt{\frac{(2xy)^2(3ab + 3x)^3}{x^3y^6}} \qquad \frac{5x^2 + 3y^2 - a^3 - b^3}{z^2 a^2 b^2}$$

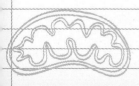

INTRODUCTION

A wise man once said that you never laugh so much
as you do when you are at school.

Actually, come to think of it, maybe he wasn't
that wise a man. Maybe he was just someone who
found school strangely hilarious. Maybe he was just
someone who started giggling uncontrollably on his
first day at primary school and didn't stop until the
day he went in to collect his GCSE and/or A-level
results. Maybe he was someone who found everything
at school so hilariously funny he literally wet himself
laughing every single day he was there and after 12
years ended up with no qualifications and a large
cleaning bill from the school. Not to mention the
cost of the enormous number of pairs of trousers,
underpants, school chairs and wooden desks that he
had ruined over the years.

Nevertheless it is true – you laugh a lot when you're
at school. There are several reasons for this.

First: usually when you start school you are very
little. And because you're so little there are probably
an awful lot of jokes that you haven't heard yet. So
most jokes will be brand new to you. You can tell a
small child a joke that is yonks old (e.g. 'Why did the
one-eyed chicken cross the road? To get to the Bird's

Eye shop') and they will think that you are a genius of comedy and should be given your own show on television straight away. Well, they might if they're familiar with the concepts of chickens, roads, Bird's Eye frozen food products and sight impairment.

Second: children will laugh a lot at almost anything. Old people hardly ever laugh. Old people will have a really good laugh if they are told the funniest joke in the world or watch the funniest film ever made. Children will laugh several thousand times more than this if they just see a friend from their class shortly after that friend has had their hair cut. If someone in their class does the most embarrassing thing possible at school and calls their teacher 'mummy' or 'daddy', their laughter will probably not die down for several years.

Third: there are often lots of stern-faced teachers pacing sternly around at school sternly telling you not to laugh at things. And if there's one thing guaranteed to make a funny thing even funnier than it was to begin with, it's a stern-faced person sternly standing over you, sternly telling you that you must not under any circumstances laugh at the funny thing you have just heard, seen and/or smelled.

$$\left(\sin\frac{\pi x}{L} - \sin\frac{3\pi x}{L}\right) \quad n=3: \omega_2 = \frac{2}{L}\sin^2\frac{3\pi x}{L};$$

So welcome to this little collection of some of the greatest jokes that have been shared in classrooms through the decades.

Don't forget, though, that the corniest, oldest jokes will be significantly funnier to you if you are a school pupil when you hear them. If you are unfortunately a bit too old for school, it may be a good time to book yourself back in as a mature pupil.

Then not only will you be able to do some of those much-needed GCSE re-sits, you'll be able to enjoy *Best Ever Classroom Jokes* in its natural environment.

THE SCHOOL SONG

God made the bees,
The bees make the honey,
We do all the work
And teacher gets the money.

THE FIRST DAY
AT SCHOOL

Henry comes home from his first day at school.
His mum asks him, 'What did you learn at school
today?'
**'Not enough,' says Henry, 'I've got to go back
tomorrow.'**

Freddie gets home from his first day at school and his
mum asks him, 'What did they teach you today?'
'They taught us how to write,' says Freddie.
'Ooo,' says mum. 'That's very clever. So what did you
write?'
**'I don't know,' says Freddie. 'They haven't
taught us to read yet.'**

The teacher asks the class, 'Who can remember the
first thing you learned when you first came to school?'
**Lily answers, 'How to speak without moving
my lips.'**

Ollie gets home from his first day at school and his mum asks him, 'How did it go?'
'OK,' says Ollie, 'except there was some person there called "teacher" who kept spoiling our fun.'

A new teacher tries doing a psychology experiment with her class.
'OK,' she says, 'I want everyone who thinks they're stupid to stand up!'
Nobody stands up at first but then after a few moments little Jayden stands up.
'Jayden!' says the teacher. 'You don't think you're stupid do you?'
'No, not really,' says Jayden. 'I just didn't like to see you standing there all by yourself!'

A teacher goes round the class getting to know her new pupils on the first day of school.
She asks Ava, 'What does your daddy do?'
'Whatever Mummy tells him,' says Ava.

ENGLISH LESSON

How many letters are there in the alphabet?
Eleven. Count them if you don't believe me.
THE ALPHABET.

What is found at the end of everything?
The letter 'G'.

The English teacher asks Lucas about the alphabet.
'Lucas,' she says, 'What comes after "O"?'
'Is it "Yeah"?' says Lucas.

The class are being taught the alphabet.
'Who can tell me what comes after "G"?'
asks the teacher.
A little boy puts his hand up and says, 'Whizz!'

The English teacher asks Bobby to come up with a sentence starting with "I".'

'I is …' says Bobby, but the teacher interrupts.

'No, no, no,' says the teacher. 'What have I told you before!? It's never "I is"! It's always "I am"! *Now* do you understand!?'

'Yes,' says Bobby and continues, 'I am the ninth letter of the alphabet.'

Name four days of the week that start with the letter 'T'?

Tuesday, Thursday, Today and Tomorrow.

Name seven days of the week that begin with 'N'.

Next Monday, next Tuesday, next Wednesday …

When does 'B' come after 'U'?

When you steal its honey.

What goes, 'Oh! Oh! Oh!'

Father Christmas walking backwards.

What word will make you sick if you take away the first letter?

Music.

Where do all the letters sleep?
In the alphabed.

Supercalifragilisticexpialidocious is a very long word.
How do you spell it?
I-T.

What word is always spelled incorrectly?
I-N-C-O-R-R-E-C-T-L-Y.

The English teacher asks Alice if she can spell
'caterpillar'.
'How much time do I have?' asks Alice.
'What difference does that make?' asks the teacher.
**'Well,' says Alice, 'if I could wait till he
changes into a butterfly, I can spell that.'**

The English teacher asks Holly, 'Do you know how to
spell banana?'
**'I do,' says Holly. 'But I'm just not sure when
to stop.'**

The teacher says to Simon, 'Simon, can you work out what your name would be if it was spelled backwards?'

'No Mis,' says Simon.

'That's correct. Excellent work,' says the teacher.

Spell the word 'ghost' out loud. Now spell the word 'most' out loud. Now spell the word 'roast' out loud. **OK. Now tell me – what is it you put in a toaster?**

'Toast!'

No! You don't put toast in a toaster! You put bread in a toaster!

Spell the word 'pots' out loud, three times in a row. **OK. Now tell me what you do when you get to a green traffic light?**

Stop

Wrong again! Green means 'go'!

The English teacher asks Lauren what she is writing.

'I'm writing a letter to myself,' says Lauren.

'Oh yes?' says the teacher. 'And what does it say?'

'I don't know yet,' says Lauren, 'I'll tell you tomorrow when I get it in the post.'

The class are handing in their homework. The teacher asks one little girl, 'What did you write your essay on, Lucy?'
'A piece of paper in my English book,' says Lucy.

The English teacher asks Mary, 'What are you reading?'
'I don't know,' says Mary.
'But you were reading out loud,' says the teacher.
'I know,' says Mary. 'But I wasn't listening.'

The teacher asks the class, 'What is the plural of man?'
Emily answers, 'Men.'
'Very good,' says the teacher and then asks, 'So, does anyone know the plural of child?'
'Yes,' says Ethan. 'Twins!'

What does an educated owl say?
To-wit-to-whom.

What is the difference between a cat and a comma?
A cat has claws at the end of its paws. A comma has its pause at the end of a clause.

What is the longest punctuation mark in the world?
The hundred-yard dash.

What starts with P, ends with E and
has a million letters in it?
Post Office.

What word has three syllables but only one letter?
Envelope.

Which is the longest word in the dictionary?
'Smiles' – there's a mile between each 's'!

The English teacher says, 'Who can tell me the
longest sentence they can think of?'
'Life imprisonment,' says Harry.

What starts with T, ends with T and is full of T?
A teapot.

Exam question: Use the word 'fascinate' in a
sentence.
**Pupil's answer: My dad has a coat with nine
buttons but he's so fat, he's only able to
fascinate.**

The English teacher asks Sophie to explain the difference in meaning between 'sufficient' and 'enough'.
'That's easy,' says Sophie, 'if my mother gives me some cake I get sufficient, but if I help myself I get enough.'

Exam question: Use the word 'diploma' in a sentence.
Pupil's answer: Our pipes were leaking so my dad called diploma.

Exam question: Use the word 'information' in a sentence.
Pupil's answer: **When they go south in winter ducks sometimes fly information.**

Define the difference between unlawful and illegal?
Unlawful means against the law and illegal is a sick bird.

Exam question: What does the word 'benign' mean?
Pupil's answer: Benign is what you are after you be eight.

$$\frac{x^2 - y^2}{\sqrt{z}} = 2\sqrt{\frac{(x^2 - y^2)(3z + 2z - y^3)}{a^2 + b^2}}$$

Exam question: What is an autobiography?
Pupil's answer: It is the life story of a car.

The English teacher asks Zoe, 'Can you use the word "aftermath" in a sentence?'
'Yes,' says Zoe, 'I always feel really sleepy after math class.'

Exam question: Use the word 'judicious' in a sentence.
Pupil's answer: Hands that judicious can be as soft as your face with mild green Fairy Liquid.

The teacher asks the class to use the word 'pregnant' in a sentence.
Jasmine puts her hand up and gives the answer: 'The pregnant fireman climbed down his ladder out of the burning building.'
The teacher is confused. 'Do you know what the word "pregnant" means?' she asks.
'Yes, miss,' says Jasmine. 'It means "carrying a child".'

'Archie,' says the teacher, 'can you define the word "procrastination" for me?'

'Can I answer that question tomorrow?' asks Archie.

The English teacher wants to stop her class using slang and says, 'There are two words I simply will not tolerate in my class. One is "gross" and the other is "cool".'

'Wow,' says one of the children. 'So can you tell us what the two words are?'

The English teacher goes round the class asking the children to give the opposites of diffcrent words.

'What is the opposite of sadness?' asks the teacher.

'Happiness, sir,' says Maria.

'Good,' says the teacher. 'And what is the opposite of ecstasy?'

'Misery, sir,' says Rebecca.

'Excellent,' says the teacher. 'And what is the opposite of woe?'

'Gee up,' says Stanley.

The English teacher asks, 'Callum, can you give me an example of a double negative?'
'But I don't know none,' says Callum.
'That's correct. Well done, Callum,' says the teacher.

The teacher asks Zac, 'Where is your pencil?'
'I ain't got none,' says Zac.
'Zac!' says the teacher. 'I've told you that is not the way to speak and that you must learn to express yourself properly. Listen carefully: "I do not have a pencil. You do not have a pencil. They do not have a pencil. We do not have pencils?" Do you understand now?'
'Yes I do,' says Zac. 'Someone's nicking all the flipping pencils!'

The teacher asks Sam, 'If "can't" is short for "cannot", what is "don't" short for?'
'Is it "doughnut"?' asks Sam.

The English teacher asks, 'Who can name three collective nouns?'
'I can,' says Sam. 'A waste-paper basket, a vacuum cleaner and a bin lorry.'

The English teacher gives his class a short written assignment. He asks them to describe themselves in ten words or less.
One boy just writes, 'Succinct.'

The English teacher tells Harry, 'Your poem is the worst that I've seen. It's ungrammatical, it's rude and it contains some disgusting language. I'm going to write a letter to your father about it.'
'I don't think that's going to help,' says Harry. 'He's the one who wrote it.'

What's the difference between a teacher and a book?
You can shut a book up.

Knock, knock.
Who's there?
Rita.
Rita who?
Rita book, you might learn something!

What noise does a frog make in the library?
Read-it, read-it, read-it.

The English teacher asks Jamie, 'Have you read any Shakespeare?'
'No,' says Jamie.
'Have you read any Dickens?' asks the teacher.
'No,' says Jamie.
'This isn't very good,' says the teacher. 'Have you read anything?'
'Yes, I have,' says Jamie. 'I've red hair.'

What's the difference between a television set and a newspaper?
Have you ever tried swatting a fly with a television set?

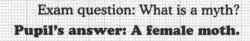

Exam question: What is a myth?
Pupil's answer: A female moth.

A primary teacher is reading the story of the three little pigs to her class.

She reads how the first little pig goes to get some material to build his house and asks the class, 'Where do you think the little pig went to get the things to build his house?'

Hannah puts her hand up and says, 'He went to a shop.'

'Very good,' says the teacher, 'and what do you think he said when he went to the shop?'

Jessica puts her hand up and says, 'Do you have any straw to build my house, please?'

'Very good,' says the teacher, 'and what do you think the shopkeeper said?'

Nathan puts his hand up and says, 'Aaaaaagh! It's a talking pig!'

The English teacher asks the class to write about a recent exciting event that has happened to them.
Later the teacher asks Callum to read out his story.
'My daddy fell down the well last week,' reads Callum.
'Oh my goodness,' says the teacher. 'So is your father all right now?'
'I think he must be,' says Callum. 'He stopped yelling for help yesterday.'

The English teacher tells the class to write an essay about their pets and it has to be no less than 500 words long.
At the end of the lesson, she collects the papers and finds one boy has written:
'Last night my dad went to the door to call our cat in. "Kitty, kitty, kitty," he called. "Kitty, kitty, kitty, kitty, kitty, kitty, kitty, kitty, kitty ..."'

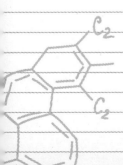

NATURE STUDY

What did one caterpillar say to the other caterpillar when he saw a butterfly fly overhead?

'You'll never get me up in one of those things!'

What did the snail say when it sat on top of the tortoise?

'Wheeeeeeeeee!'

What do you call a deer with no eyes?

No-eyed deer.

What do you call a deer with no eyes AND no legs?

Still no-eyed deer.

What do you call a film about mallards?

A duckumentary.

What do you call a fly with no wings?

A walk.

What do you call a guy with six rabbits up his bum?
Warren.

What do you call a turtle that can fly?
A shell-icopter.

What do you get if you cross a bullet
and a tree with no leaves?
A cartridge in a bare tree.

What do you get if you cross a caterpillar
and a parrot?
A walkie-talkie.

What do you get if you cross a daffodil
with a crocodile?
**I'm not sure, but if I were you I
wouldn't try sniffing it.**

What do you get if you cross a firefly and a moth?
An insect that can find its way round in a dark wardrobe.

What do you get if you cross a ghost
and a couple of bees?
A pair of boo-bees.

What do you get if you cross a porcupine
with a sheep?
An animal that can knit itself into a jumper.

What do you get if you cross a mole with a hedgehog?
A tunnel that leaks.

What does a hedgehog like to eat?
Prickled onions.

What do you get if you cross a spider
and an elephant?
**I'm not sure but if you see one walking across
the ceiling you'd better get out of the way
before it drops on you.**

What do you get if you cross a strawberry
with a road?
A traffic jam.

What do you get if you cross a wolf and an egg?
A hairy omelette.

What do you get if you cross an anthill
with a packet of seeds?
Ants in your plants.

What happens to illegally parked frogs?
They get toad away.

What is the worst thing that can happen
to a hibernating bat?
Diarrhoea.

What lies on the ground 100 feet in the air?
A dead caterpillar.

What's the world's most useful owl?
The tea t-owl.

Why do bees hum?
Because they don't know the words.

Why do birds fly south for the winter?
It's easier than walking.

A monkey, a squirrel and a bird all go racing to the
top of a coconut tree. Which of them will get to the
top of the tree and pick themselves a banana first?
**None of them. You don't get bananas from
coconut trees.**

Did you hear about the two bedbugs who fell in love?
They got married in the spring.

What did the stupid person do to get rid
of the flea in his ear?
He got a gun and shot it.

Did you hear about the two silkworms
who had a race?
It ended in a tie.

Have you heard the joke about the skunk?
It stinks!

How do you stop a skunk from smelling?
Put a clothes peg on its nose.

How does a flea get from place to place?
By itch-hiking.

The peacock is a bird that does not lay eggs.
So where do baby peacocks come from?
From the peahen who lays the eggs.

HISTORY LESSON

Exam question: What does BC stand for?

Pupil's answer: Before computers.

What does AD mean?

It's the letter that comes between AC and AE.

Which king was round, brown and shiny?

William the Conker.

Which king was purple, oval and squashy?

Alfred the Grape.

Which king invented the mobile phone network?

William of Orange.

Which king drank the most?

Charles the Thirst.

Which king had to have 87.5 per cent
of his entire body removed?

Henry the Eighth.

What happens to deposed kings?
They get throne away.

What happened when the wheel was invented?
It caused a revolution.

What sort of music do Egyptian mummies like?
Wrap music.

What was the most popular type of flowers
in ancient Egypt?
Chrysanthemummies!

How did doorbells work in Ancient Egypt?
You just used to toot-an-come-in.

The history teacher is showing her class round the
local museum. She leads them to see an Ancient
Egyptian mummy and says, 'Next to this exhibit it
says 1286 BC. What do you think that means?'
**Chloe puts her hand up and asks, 'Is that the
registration of the car that ran him over?'**

The history teacher asks her class if they can tell her where Hadrian's Wall was built.

Hugo puts his hand up and asks, 'Is it round Hadrian's garden?'

Exam question: What is a forum?

Pupil's answer: It's a two-um plus a two-um.

The history teacher asks the class, 'When was Rome built?'

'At night,' answers Matthew.

'What do you mean, "at night"?' asks the teacher.

'It must have been,' says Matthew. 'Because my dad always says that Rome wasn't built in a day.'

The history teacher asks, 'What do you think the Ancient Romans considered to be their greatest achievement?'

'Being able to speak Latin,' says Dexter.

$$\sqrt{\frac{a^2 + \frac{1}{3}b^x}{y^2}} \cdot \frac{z^3}{a^0} = \frac{\left(a^2 + b^2 + x^2 + y^2\right)\left(x^3 - b^3\right)}{\sqrt{3x - 2y^3 - z^2}}$$

How did the Roman cannibal feel
about his mother-in-law?
Gladiator.

How was the Roman Empire cut in half?
With a pair of Caesars.

How did the Dark Ages get their name?
**Because it was a time when there were lots of
knights.**

How did Vikings send secret messages?
By Norse code.

Which king invented the fireplace?
Alfred the Grate!

Who invented the round table for King Arthur?
Sir Cumference.

Where was the Magna Carta signed?
At the bottom!

Who was the Black Prince?
He was the son of Old King Cole.

Exam question: Spanish explorers travelled the world using galleons. What is a galleon?
Pupil's answer: It's an amount of fuel, e.g. Christopher Columbus' ship did 40 miles to the galleon.

Who invented the pen?
The Inkas.

Why did Henry VIII put skittles on his lawn?
He wanted to take Anne Boleyn.

A teacher is testing her class on the Tudor kings and queens of Great Britain. 'Who followed Edward VI?' asks the teacher.

'Mary!' says a girl at the front of the class.

'Very good,' says the teacher. 'And who followed Mary?'

'Her little lamb,' says a boy at the back.

What have Winnie the Pooh and Ivan the Terrible got in common?

They both have the same middle name.

'When did Henry VIII die?' asks the teacher.

'A few days before they buried him,' says Felix.

Where did the pilgrims land when they came to America?

On their feet.

Where do pirates do their shopping?

Aaaaaaaaaarrrrrrrr-gos.

Why do pirates take so long to learn the alphabet?

Because they always end up spending years at 'C'.

How much will a pirate pay to get his ears pierced?
A buck-an-ear.

What rating did they give the new pirate movie?
aRRRgh!

The history teacher is telling the class about
American history and how, when he was a boy, the
first US president George Washington chopped down
his father's cherry tree but then went and admitted it.
The teacher asks the class, 'Who can tell me why
George Washington's father didn't punish him?'
**Aidan puts his hand up and says, 'Because he
still had the axe in his hand?'**

Exam question: Who succeeded the first
President of the USA?
**Pupil's answer: The second
President of the USA.**

Exam question: During which battle was
Lord Nelson killed?
Pupil's answer: His last one.

Exam question: When was Napoleon born?
Pupil's answer: On his birthday.

Where did Napoleon keep his armies?
Up his sleevies.

The history teacher asks Katie,
'How long did Queen Victoria live?'
'All her life,' says Katie.

Exam question: Who was Charles Darwin?
**Pupil's answer: Charles Darwin was a naturist
who wrote the *Organ of the Species*.**

Exam question: Why was Karl Marx buried
in Highgate cemetery?
Pupil's answer: Because he was dead.

Why did cowboys ride horses?
Because they were too heavy to carry.

Who wears a mask and works in a bank?
The Loan Arranger.

Which Western hero was created in a science lab?
The Clone Ranger.

Knock, knock.
Who's there?
Ya!
Ya who?
I didn't know you were a cowboy.

What finally made the invention of the
first telephone useful to people?
The invention of the second telephone.

The history teacher asks Orla, 'What do you think would be the difference between the death rate today and the death rate 100 years ago?'
'It would be exactly the same, wouldn't it?' says Orla. **'One per person.'**

What happens if you cross a pigeon and a general?
You get a military coo.

Why does history keep repeating itself?
Because the class wasn't listening the first time.

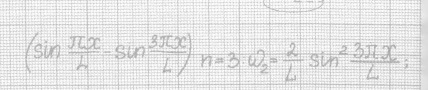

NAUGHTY BEHAVIOUR IN CLASS

The teacher gets cross with Liam.
'You aren't paying attention to me, are you, Liam?'
says the teacher. 'Are you having trouble hearing?'
**'No, sir,' says Liam. 'I'm having trouble
listening.'**

Why is whispering not permitted in class?
Because it's not aloud.

The teacher is getting fed up with Jake's behaviour in
class.
'Honestly, Jake,' says the teacher, 'every time I
turn round I catch you doing something you're not
supposed to be doing. How are we going to stop this
happening?'
**'Well,' says Jake, 'you could try telling me
every time you're about to turn round.'**

A teacher asks Dylan, 'Why are you never able to
answer any of my questions?'
**'Look on the bright side,' says Dylan. 'If I
could there wouldn't be any need for me to
come to school any more and then you'd be
out of a job!'**

Freddie comes home from school with a black eye. 'What happened to your eye?' asks his mum. 'I thought you knew that good boys don't fight.'

'I know,' says Freddie. 'The problem was that I thought Ben was a good boy but then when I hit him it turned out he wasn't.'

The teacher notices William staring out of the window during the English lesson.

'William,' she says, 'can you give me two pronouns?'

William looks round and says, 'Who? Me?'

'That's right. Very good,' says the teacher.

The teacher says to Alice, 'Didn't you hear me call your name in the register?'

'Yes, sir,' says Alice. 'But yesterday you told me not to answer you back.'

The teacher spots one of the boys in her class pulling a funny face.

'Billy,' the teacher tells him, 'when I was little I was told that if I pulled a funny face, the wind would change and my face would get stuck like that.'

'Well,' says Billy, 'you can't say you weren't warned.'

$$\sqrt[3]{\frac{(2xy)^3 \cdot (3ab+3x)^3}{y^3}} = \frac{5x^3+3y-a-b}{z^3 a^4 b^3} \qquad \frac{x^4-y^3}{\sqrt{z^3}} \quad 2\sqrt{\frac{(x^3-y^6)(3z+2)}{a^3+b^6}}$$

$$\sqrt[3]{\frac{(2xy)^3 \cdot (3ab+3x)^3}{y^3}} \qquad \frac{5x^2+3y^3-a^3 \cdot b^7}{z^2 a^2 b^2}$$

The teacher tells Connor, 'Don't you know, you can't sleep in my class.'

'I know,' says Connor. 'But perhaps if you tried speaking a bit more quietly ...'

The maths teacher notices that Leah isn't paying attention.

'Leah!' she calls. 'What are 5 and 28 and 41 and 71?'

'Channel 5, E4, Food Network and CBeebies,' says Leah.

Did you hear about the maths teacher who confiscated a rubber-band gun from one of the pupils in his class?

He said it was a weapon of math disruption.

What did the inflatable teacher say to the inflatable boy who took a pin to his inflatable school?

You've let me down, you've let yourself down, but worst of all you've let the entire school down.

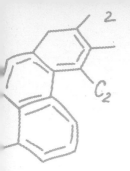

FOOD SCIENCE

Knock, knock.
Who's there?
Justin.
Justin who?
Just in time for dinner.

Did you hear about the dinner lady
who got an electric shock?
**She stepped on a bun and a
current went up her leg.**

How do you know cooks are cruel?
**Every day they beat the eggs and
whip the cream.**

Did you hear about the man who tried to eat a clock?
He found it very time-consuming.

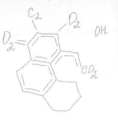

How does Batman's mum call him in for his tea?
**Dinner dinner dinner dinner, dinner
dinner dinner dinner, dinner dinner
dinner dinner, Batman!**

Knock, knock.
Who's there?
Arthur.
Arthur who?
Arthur any biscuits in the cupboard?

Did you hear about the race between the lettuce,
the tomato and the tap?
**The lettuce was ahead, the tomato couldn't
ketchup, but the tap just kept on running.**

Exam question: Name the four seasons.
**Pupil's answer: Salt, pepper,
mustard and vinegar.**

Exam question: What is the best way
to delay milk turning sour?
Pupil's answer: Leave it inside the cow.

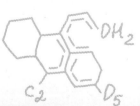

How do you make a fruit punch?
Give it some boxing lessons.

How do you make a milkshake?
Creep up behind it and shout, 'Boo!'

How do you make an apple crumble?
Keep hitting it with a mallet.

How do you make an artichoke?
Strangle it.

Have you heard the joke about the butter?
**I'd better not tell you, you'll only
spread it around.**

Have you heard the joke about the coffee?
It's hot stuff.

Have you heard the joke about the dropped egg?
It cracks me up every time.

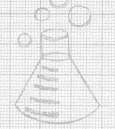

Have you heard the song about the tortilla?
Actually, it's more of a rap.

How do we know carrots are good for your eyesight?
You've never seen a rabbit with glasses, have you?

Why was the little strawberry sad?
Because his mummy was in a jam.

Why did the chewing gum cross the road?
It was stuck to the chicken's foot.

How do you eat an elephant?
One bite at a time.

How do you know if there is an elephant in your fridge?
Footprints in the butter.

How do you know if there are
two elephants in your fridge?
Two sets of footprints in the butter.

How do you know if there are three
elephants in your fridge?
You can't get the fridge door closed.

How do you get an elephant in a refrigerator?
**1. Open the door. 2. Put the elephant in.
3. Close the door.**

How do you get a giraffe in a refrigerator?
**1. Open the door. 2. Remove the elephant.
3. Put the giraffe in. 4. Close the door.**

What do elephants have for lunch?
Forty minutes, the same as everyone else.

Knock, knock.
Who's there?
Banana.
Banana who?
Knock, knock.
Who's there?
Banana.
Banana who?
Knock, knock.
Who's there?
Orange.
Orange who?
Orange you glad it's not another banana?

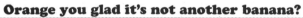

Knock, knock.
Who's there?
Lettuce.
Lettuce who?
Lettuce in, it's freezing out here!

What cheese is made backwards?
Edam.

Give me food, and I will live; give me water,
and I will die. What am I?
A fire.

What did the grape say when it was trodden on?
**It didn't say anything, it just let out
a little wine.**

What did the green grape say to the purple grape?
'Breathe, breathe!'

What did the little boy say when his mother poured
porridge all over his head?
'Mother, how can you be so gruel?'

What did the mayonnaise say to the refrigerator?
'Close the door, please, I'm dressing.'

What did the peanut say to the walnut?
Nothing. Nuts cannot talk.

What did the plate say to the saucer?
'Tonight dinner's on me.'

What do you call a fake noodle?
An impasta.

What do you call a frightened biscuit?
A cowardy-cowardy custard cream.

What do you call a girl who likes
a lot of butter
on her bread?
Marge.

What do you call a girl with a steak and
a sausage on her head?
Barbie.

What do you call a guy who likes meat,
potatoes and vegetables?
Stu.

What do you call a woman who can balance
four pints of beer on her head?
Beatrix.

What do you call a woman who can balance four
pints of beer on her head while playing snooker?
Beatrix Potter.

What do you call a woman who liquidises
fruit and vegetables?
Belinda.

What do you call the king of vegetables?
Elvis Parsley.

What do you get if you cross a birthday cake
with a tin of baked beans?
A cake that can blow its own candles out.

What do you make from baked beans and onions?
Tear gas.

What do you get if you cross a door knocker with
some courgettes, tomatoes and onion?
Rat-a-tat-a-touille.

What do you get if you cross an
elephant with an apple?
A pie that never forgets.

What do you say to a beef burger?
How now, ground cow?

What happens if you eat so much curry you pass out?
You go into a korma.

What happens if you eat yeast and shoe polish?
The next morning you'll rise and shine.

What is rhubarb?
It's a kind of celery that's gone bloodshot.

What is the difference between
roast beef and pea soup?
Most people can roast beef.

What keeps hot in the fridge?
Mustard.

What should you do for a lemon in distress?
Offer him a bit of lemonade.

What swings from cake to cake and
smells of almonds?
Tarzipan.

What type of coffee do vampires like to drink?
**Decoffinated. Anything else and
they're up all night.**

What type of nut suffers from a nasty cold?
A ca-shew!

What's a toad's favourite drink?
Croak-a cola.

What's full of sandwiches and can be
found in a French cathedral?
The lunch pack of Notre Dame.

What's made of flour, is covered in cheese and tomato
and is 182 feet tall?
The Leaning Tower of Pizza.

What's smelly, round, and laughs?
A tickled onion.

What's the best way to keep flies out of the kitchen?
**Put a pile of manure in the middle
of your living room.**

What's the difference between bogeys and beetroot?
Children will eat bogeys.

What's the main ingredient of dog biscuits?
Collie flour.

What's worse than finding a worm in your apple?
Finding half a worm.

When is it dangerous to be hit by a tomato?
When it's still in the can.

Where do you go to weigh a pie?
Somewhere over the rainbow, weigh a pie!

Why did the banana take the day off work?
Because it wasn't peeling well.

Why did the cannibal student get
expelled from school?
Because he kept buttering up the teacher.

A mum says to her son, 'Why did you just
swallow the money I gave you?'
**'Because,' says the boy, 'you told me it
was my lunch money!'**

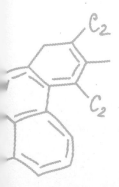

BIOLOGY LESSON

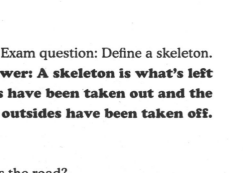

Two dads are talking.
'My son has left school and gone to medical school,' says the first.
'Oh,' says the second dad. 'So what's he studying?'
'He isn't,' says the first dad. 'They're studying him.'

Exam question: Define a skeleton.
Pupil's answer: A skeleton is what's left after the insides have been taken out and the outsides have been taken off.

Why did the skeleton cross the road?
He was trying to get to the Body Shop.

Why didn't the skeleton cross the road?
He didn't have the guts for it.

Exam question: Describe the functions
of the human spine.
**Pupil's answer: The spinal column is a big
stack of bones. The head sits on the top and
you sit on the bottom.**

Exam question: What is the fibula?
Pupil's answer: The fibula is a small lie.

What do you call a guy who has a bullet-proof skull?
Helmut.

What do you call a man with no legs?
Neil.

What do you call a man with no shins?
Tony.

What do you call a man with no arms,
no legs and no head?
Chester.

$$\left(\sin \frac{\pi x}{L} - \sin \frac{3\pi x}{L}\right) \quad n = 3 \cdot \omega_2 = \frac{2}{L} \sin^2 \frac{3\pi x}{L};$$

What do you call a man with three eyes?
Seymour.

What do you call a pig with three eyes?
A piiig.

What do you call a man who has been
attacked by a lion?
Claude.

What has a bottom at the top?
Your legs.

What has a head and a tail but no body?
A coin.

What has a neck but is unable to swallow?
A bottle.

What has a thousand legs but no feet?
Five hundred pairs of trousers.

When are your eyes not eyes?
When the wind makes them water.

What did one eye say to the other eye?
'Between you and me something smells.'

Why didn't the nose want to go to school?
He was fed up with being picked on.

Why isn't your nose 12 inches long?
Because then it would be a foot.

Exam question: Describe how blood circulates
in the human body.
**Pupil's answer: Blood flows down one leg
and comes back up the other.**

Exam question: Name the three different
types of blood vessels.
**Pupil's answer: Arteries,
veins and caterpillars.**

Exam question: What does the word 'varicose' mean?
Pupil's answer: Not very far away.

A teacher is giving a lesson on the circulation of the blood. 'Now, class,' she says. 'If I stood on my head, all the blood in my body would run into my head and my face would go red. Is that right?'
'Yes, miss,' say the class.
'So,' says the teacher, 'why is it that if I stand the right way up, the blood doesn't run into my feet and make them red?'
'Because your feet aren't empty,' says a boy at the back of the class.

Why was the student vampire so tired
in the morning?
Because he'd been up all night studying for his blood test.

Exam question: Describe what happens when the human body is immersed in water.
Pupil's answer: The phone rings.

Exam question: Describe how the lungs work.
Pupil's answer: When you breathe, you inspire. When you stop breathing, you expire.

Exam question: Describe how the main parts of the body are categorised?
Pupil's answer: The body is consisted into three parts, the brainium, the borax, and the abdominal cavity. The branium contains the brain, the borax contains the heart and lungs, and the abdominal cavity contains the five bowels, A, E, I, O and U.

What do they have to give someone who has water on the brain?
A small tap on the head.

What is the best way to determine the sex of a chromosome?
Pull down its genes.

Exam question: Explain how genetics can affect your appearance?
Pupil's answer: Genetics explains why you look like your father and if you don't, why you should.

Exam question: Give an example of a fungus and explain their characteristic features.
Pupil's answers: Mushrooms are a fungus. They always grow in damp places and that is why they look like little umbrellas.

Exam question: What are steroids used for?
Pupil's answer: Steroids are things that keep carpet in place on the stairs.

Exam question: What is a seizure?
Pupil's answer: A Roman emperor.

Exam question: What is a terminal illness?
Pupil's answer: It is when you don't feel well at the airport.

Exam question: What is meant by the term 'Caesarean Section'?
Pupil's answer: The Caesarean Section is the name of a district in Ancient Rome.

What has tracks that arrive before it does?
A train.

The science teacher is giving his class a lesson in biology. He holds up a jar of yellow liquid.
'To be a good scientist, you have to be very observant,' says the teacher. 'When you look at a jar of bodily fluid like this you have to observe its colour, smell and appearance. And that's not all ...'
And then, to the class's horror, the teacher dips into the jar and puts his finger in his mouth.
'Now I want you all to do the same,' says the teacher.
The pupils screw their faces up as they pass round the jar and they each dip their finger in and taste it.
'Very good,' says the teacher, 'except you all fail on basic observation. None of you noticed that I dipped my second finger into the jar and then put my first finger into my mouth.'

DRAMA LESSON

Did you hear about the class that did a theatrical performance about puns?
It was a play on words.

Knock, knock.
Who's there?
Radio.
Radio who?
Radio not, here I come!

Knock, knock.
Who's there?
Alison.
Alison who?
Alison to the radio.

Did you hear about the little boy who got a part in the school play and then halfway through the performance fell through a hole in the floor?
The teacher said it was just a stage he was going through.

What's the best way to kill a variety act?
Go for the juggler.

ECONOMICS LESSON

What's the quickest way to double your money?
Fold it in half.

Why is paper money worth more than loose change?
Because when you put it in your pocket you double it and when you take it out it's in creases.

Why are 1976 pennies worth more
than 1971 pennies?
Because there are 5 more of them.

Why did Robin Hood only rob the rich?
Because the poor never had anything worth stealing.

When does it rain money?
When there's change in the weather!

Have you heard about the private school where
all the pupils stink to high heaven?
You have to be filthy rich to go there.

When is the cheapest time to call your
friends long distance?
When they're not home.

What do you call a man who's in debt?
Owen.

What do you call a woman who sets fire
to any bills that arrive?
Bernadette.

What's the name of the richest bear in the world?
Winnie the Pools.

Did you hear about the man who couldn't keep
up his payments to the exorcist?
He got re-possessed.

Three budgies are sitting in a cage. One is on the top perch, one is on the middle perch and the third is on the bottom perch. Which of them owns the cage?
The one on the bottom. The others are both on higher perches.

The teacher asks his class, 'Who can tell me what happens to a car when it gets old and starts to go rusty?'
'My dad buys it,' says Tommy.

The class are discussing dressing smartly and how some poor people have holes in their clothes.
Bobby asks the teacher, 'Sir, do you have holes in your underpants?'
'Don't be so ridiculous. Of course I don't,' says the teacher.
'Really?' says Bobby. 'So how do you get your legs through them then?'

What is the difference between a well-dressed man and an exhausted dog?
One wears a suit, the other just pants.

The teacher asks the class to write a story about what they would do if they had a million pounds. Everyone starts writing apart from Isla, who hands in a completely blank sheet of paper at the end of the lesson.

'Isla,' says the teacher, 'everyone else has written several pages on what they would do if they had a million pounds but you've done absolutely nothing.'

'I know,' says Isla, 'and if I had a million pounds, that's exactly what I'd do.'

FARM VISIT

If a farmer raises wheat in dry weather, what does he raise in wet weather?
His umbrella.

What runs round a farm but never moves?
A fence.

What do you call a man who smells like a farmyard?
Barney.

Why did the scarecrow get a promotion?
The farmer had found him outstanding in his field.

What does a horse say when it steps out of the fridge?
Brrrrrrrrrrrrrrrr.

What did the pony with the sore throat say?
'I really must apologise. I am a little horse.'

Why did the horse eat with its mouth open?
It had terrible stable manners.

When does a cart come before a horse?
In the dictionary!

What goes clip?
A one-legged horse.

What do you call a donkey with three legs?
A wonkey.

What do you get if you cross a donkey with an owl?
A smart ass who knows it all.

What do you get if you cross a
pig with a Christmas tree?
A porky pine.

Where do pigs park their cars?
In a porking lot.

What do you get if you cross a dog and a sheep?
A sheep that can round itself up.

Why do white sheep eat more grass than black ones?
Because there's more of them.

Where do sheep get their wool cut?
At the baaa-bers!

What do sheep like to do on sunny days?
Invite their friends over for a baa-baa-cue.

What do you call a woman with a sheep on her head?
Baa-baa-ra.

What do you get if you cross a
chicken and a centipede?
Drumsticks for everyone.

What do you get if you cross a chicken with a bell?
An alarm cluck.

What do you get if you cross a chicken
with a cement mixer?
A brick layer.

What do you get if you cross a chicken with a zebra?
**A four-legged dinner that comes with its own
barcode.**

What do you call a haunted chicken?
A poultry-geist.

Why wasn't the chicken able to find her eggs?
She had mislaid them.

If a cockerel was sitting on your roof and it laid an
egg, would it roll off to the left or to the right?
Neither. Cockerels don't lay eggs.

What did the chicken say after laying a square egg?
'Ouch!'

Have you heard the joke about the cows?
Don't worry. It's udder nonsense.

Why do cows have to wear bells?
Because their horns don't work.

Why do cows lie down when it rains?
They want to keep each udder dry.

Why did the cow jump over the moon?
Because the farmer had cold hands.

Where does a cow stay when she goes on holiday?
In a moo-tel.

Where do cows go on a Saturday night?
The moo-vies!

What's the difference between a duck and a cow?
They both swim, except for the cow.

What goes moo, baa, oink, woof, quack?
A multi-lingual cow.

What has four legs and says, 'Boo'?
A cow with a cold.

What goes 'oooooooooooooooo!'
A cow with no lips.

What do you call a cow sitting
in a car spying on another cow?
A steak out.

What do you get if you cross a
cow with a trampoline?
Milkshake!

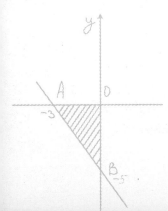

What do you get if you cross a cow and a camel?
A milkshake with lumps.

What do you get if you cross a cow,
a sheep, and a goat?
The milky baa kid!

Two cows are standing in a field.
One says to the other, 'Are you worried about this
Mad Cow Disease?'
'No, why should I be?' says the second.
'I'm a chicken.'

Two cows are standing in a field.
One says, 'Moo.'
**'That's amazing,' says the second cow. 'I was
about to say exactly the same thing.'**

Knock, knock.
Who's there?
Interrupting cow.
Interrupting c—
Mooo!

MATHS LESSON

If two's company, and three's a crowd,
what are four and five?
Nine.

How do you make seven even?
Take away the 's'.

Why was six unhappy?
Because seven eight nine.

How much dirt is there in a 2 foot
by 3 foot hole?
None. It's a hole.

If there are three apples and you took away two,
how many do you have?
Two. I told you – you just took away two.

If I have two fish and one of them drowns,
how many do I have left?
Two. Fish don't drown.

If it took eight men ten hours to build a wall, how
long would it take four men to build it?
**They don't have to. The eight men have
already done it.**

The teacher asks, 'If I had five coconuts and I gave
you three, how many would I have left?'
'I don't know,' says Lucy.
'Why not?' asks the teacher.
**'Our last maths teacher taught us in apples
and oranges,' says Lucy.**

The maths teacher gives Violet a problem.
'Say there were five people and you had four apples,
how would you divide them up?'
**'Well,' says Violet, 'I'd ask someone to go and
find a knife.'**
'Very good,' says the teacher. 'And then what?'
**'And then whoever was stupid enough to go
wouldn't get an apple,' says Violet.**

Exam question: What is a right angle?
Pupil's answer: A right angle is 90 degrees Fahrenheit.

How does a mathematician solve the problem of constipation?
He sits down and works it out with a pencil.

How many sides does a circle have?
Two – an inside and an outside.

What's the longest piece of furniture in the world?
The multiplication table.

The maths class is doing percentages. 'If there are ten questions on a test,' says the teacher, 'and you get ten right, what do you get?'
'Accused of cheating,' says Jackson.

The maths teacher asks Frankie, 'Tell me how you would find the square root of 144?'

'Well,' says Frankie, 'probably what I'd do is find someone who's cleverer than I am and I'd ask them.'

The maths teacher asks Joshua, 'If eggs are one pound for a dozen and you had 40p, how many eggs would you be able to get?'

'None,' says Joshua.

'What do you mean "none"?' asks the teacher.

'Well,' says Joshua, 'if I had 40p I'd spend it on a bag of crisps instead.'

The teacher asks his class, 'If you got £10 from ten people, what would you have?'

Eric puts his hand up and answers, 'A new bike!'

The teacher asks Lucas, 'Can you count to ten?'

'Yes I can,' says Lucas. 'One, two, three, four, five, six, seven, eight, nine, ten.'

'Very good,' says the teacher. 'And are you able to do any more after ten?'

'Yes,' says Lucas. 'Jack, Queen, King.'

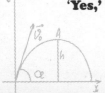

The teacher asks Phoebe, 'If there were seven flies on my desk and I whacked one of them with my ruler, how many would be left?'
'Just the squashed one,' says Phoebe.

The teacher asks the class, 'What does it mean when we say we need to make little things count?'
Alice puts her hand up and says, 'Does it mean we should teach arithmetic to toddlers?'

The teacher gives Kevin a maths problem.
'If you had £15 in one pocket and £27 in the other pocket, what would you have?'
'Somebody else's trousers on,' says Kevin.

The teacher says to Elijah, 'If I had nine apples and 12 children, how would I divide the apples equally?'
'You could cook them and put them in 12 apple pies,' says Elijah.

There are ten cats in a boat. One cat jumped out of the boat. How many cats were left?
None, they were all copycats.

$$y = \cos\frac{t}{2} \int \frac{\sqrt{x^4 - a^2}}{x^2} \, dx \quad \frac{\cos x}{2} \quad \frac{3\pi x}{L} \quad \Delta T = E e^2$$

$$\left(\sin\frac{\pi x}{L} - \sin\frac{3\pi x}{L} \right) n = 3 \quad \omega_2 = \frac{2}{L} \sin^2\frac{3\pi x}{L}$$

There are three apples which have to be shared between two sons and two fathers. Each of them gets their own apple. How is this possible?
There are only three people: one son, one father and one grandfather.

What did the first maths book say to the second maths book?
'Stop bothering me, I've got my own problems.'

What do you get if you divide the circumference of an apple by its diameter?
Apple pi.

What gets smaller the more you put into it?
A hole in the ground.

What is half of infinity?
Nity.

What's a polygon?
A dead parrot.

When does 10 + 3 = 1?
On a clock.

Why is it dangerous to do maths in the jungle?
Because if you add four plus four you get ate!

Why should you never mention the
number 288 in front of anyone?
It's two gross!

Why was it painful for the geometry teacher to walk?
She'd had an accident and broken her angle.

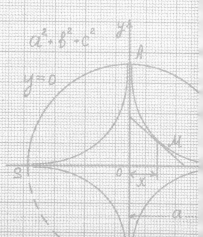

Jake is doing badly in maths. His mum and dad decide there's only one thing for it. They send him to the ultra-strict local Catholic school. Soon his maths grades start improving rapidly.

'We're really pleased with your progress,' Mum tells Jake. 'But how were they able to get you to do maths at this school when the last school couldn't?'

'The Catholics are much stricter about maths,' says Jake. 'As soon as I walked in and saw the statue of the guy nailed to a giant plus-sign, I knew they meant business.'

The maths teacher asks Eric, 'If you multiply 8 by 12, divide the total by 4 and add 31 what would you end up with?'

'The wrong answer,' says Eric.

The maths teacher says to Luke, 'If I bought 50 doughnuts for one pound what does that mean that each of them would be?'

'Stale,' says Luke, 'if they were selling them off that cheap.'

The maths teacher is having difficulty getting Martha to do basic sums.

'Martha,' says the teacher, 'if I gave you two rabbits and then another two rabbits and then another two rabbits, how many rabbits would you have?

'Seven,' says Martha.

'No, that's not right,' says the teacher. 'Let's try again. If I gave you two rabbits and then two more rabbits, how many rabbits would you have?'

'Five,' says Martha.

'Wrong again. Let's try a different one,' says the teacher. 'If I gave you two apples and two apples and another two apples, how many apples would you have?'

'Six,' says Martha.

'That's better,' says teacher. 'So what about if gave you two rabbits and then another two rabbits, how many rabbits would you have?'

'Five,' says Martha.

'What do you mean?' says the teacher crossly. 'How do you work out that two lots of two rabbits is five?'

'It isn't,' says Martha, 'but then I have to add on the one I've already got at home.'

The maths teacher says, 'OK, Sadie, tell me what you would get if you divide 88 by four and multiply the result by seven.'

'A headache, sir,' says Sadie.

The maths teacher sets Clara a different problem.
'Can you work out how many seconds there are in an
entire year?' asks the teacher.
'Yes,' says Clara. 'There's 12.'
'How do you work that out?' asks the teacher.
**'Well,' says Clara, 'there's the second of
January, the second of February, the second of
March...'**

The maths teacher sets his class a problem. 'Imagine
there are a dozen sheep. Six of them jump over a
fence. How many would be left?'
'None,' says Jasper.
'What do you mean "none"?' says the teacher. 'You
don't know your arithmetic.'
**'No, sir,' says Jasper, 'you don't know your
sheep. When one goes, they all go.'**

The maths teacher tells the class, 'If I had nine
oranges in one hand and eight apples in the other
hand, what would I have?'
**Connor puts his hand up and says,
'Unnaturally large hands, sir.'**

The maths teacher tries to explain addition to one of the little boys in her class.

'Toby, if I laid two eggs over there and two eggs over here, how many would I have?'

'I'm not sure at the moment,' says Toby. 'I'll have to see you do it first.'

The teacher asks Alex, 'Which month has 28 days?'

'All of them,' says Alex.

The teacher asks Lottie, 'If you had one pound and you asked your dad for ten more, how much would you have?'

'One pound,' says Lottie.

'Really?' says the teacher. 'Are you quite sure?'

'Yes,' says Lottie. 'My dad would never give me ten pounds.'

The teacher asks Oscar, 'Are you any good at maths?'

'Yes and no,' says Oscar.

'What do you mean, "yes and no"?'
asks the teacher.

'Yes,' says Oscar, 'I am no good at maths.'

The teacher asks Tristan, 'How much is half of eight?'
'Up and down or across?' asks Tristan.
'What do you mean?' asks the teacher.
'Well,' says Tristan, 'Half of eight up and down is three and across the middle is a zero.'

The teacher gives the class a maths problem.
'OK,' says the teacher. 'Imagine your dad earned £1,000 this week and on Friday he gives your mother half. What would your mum then have?'
Alfie puts his hand up and answers, 'A heart attack, miss.'

The teacher tells the class, 'Now listen, everyone. When I ask a question, I want you to all answer at once. So how much is six plus four?'
'At once!' reply the class together.

PLAYTIME

Knock, knock.
Who's there?
Keanu.
Keanu who?
Keanu come out to play?

What do you call a girl who like to
play hide-and-seek?
Heidi.

Why did the chicken cross the park?
To get to the other slide.

Have you heard about the boy who went to school
and his friends came up and said, 'Let's play tick!'
And then they infested him with ticks.

Have you heard the joke about the playing cards?
It's no big deal.

Two men play seven games of dominos.
Each of the men wins an equal
number of games and none of their
games ends in a draw. How is it possible?
**The two men weren't playing
against each other.**

How do you get rid of a boomerang?
Throw it down a one-way street.

What do you call a boomerang that
will not come back?
A stick.

Billy, Johnny and Tommy are walking through a forest. They find a playground which has a slide in the middle.

A fairy appears and tells them this is a magic slide. If they shout the name of something as they slide down, they will land at the bottom of the slide in a big pile of the thing they just shouted.

Billy slides down first and shouts, 'Ice cream!' as he goes.

Sure enough, he lands in a big pile of strawberry ice cream at the bottom of the slide.

Next, Johnny goes on the slide and shouts, 'Chocolate cake!' as he slides down.

Again, he lands in an enormous, lovely chocolate cake.

Then it's Tommy's go.

Unfortunately, Tommy forgets what he's supposed to shout as he goes down the slide and gets excited and just yells, 'Weeeeeeeeeeeeeee!'

A moment later there's the sound of a horrible splosh.

ART AND
DESIGN LESSON

What kind of coat has no buttons
and you put it on wet?
A coat of paint.

What gets taken before you even get it?
Your picture.

Why did the picture have to go to jail?
Because it had been framed.

What did the pencil sharpener say to the pencil?
**Will you stop going round and round in circles
and just get to the point.**

What do you call a man who people
keep hanging pictures on?
Wally.

What do you call a man who's been covered
in paint and hung up on the wall?
Art.

The teacher is going round looking at the class
drawing.
She says to one little girl, 'Katy, I told the class to
draw a horse and cart, but you have only drawn a
horse!'
**'That's right, miss,' says Katy. 'And now the
horse will draw the cart!'**

A nursery-school teacher is watching her class while
they draw. She walks around to see each child's
drawing and comes to little Jenny, who is filling a
piece of paper with her picture.
The teacher asks, 'What are you drawing, Jenny?'
'I'm drawing God,' says Jenny.
'Very good,' says the teacher, 'but no one really knows
what God looks like, do they?'
'They will in a minute,' says Jenny.

HA HA HA

The teacher is going round looking at the class drawing.

She says to one little boy, 'Josh, I asked you to draw a cow eating some grass. But you've only drawn a cow.'

'I did draw the grass,' says Josh, 'but you took so long to get here, the cow ate it.'

Did you hear about the little boy who didn't tell his teacher he'd been eating glue during the art lesson?

His lips were sealed.

What's black and white and red all over?

A newspaper.

What else is black and white and red all over?

A Dalmatian with sunburn.

What else is black and white and red all over?

An embarrassed penguin.

What goes black, white, black, white, black, white, black, white?

A penguin rolling down a hill.

What goes black, white, yellow, black, white,
yellow, black, white, yellow, black, white, yellow?
**A penguin rolling down a hill with
a daffodil in its mouth.**

What's black and white and blue all over?
A zebra on a cold day.

What's black and white and makes a lot of noise?
A zebra with a drum kit.

What's black and white and goes round and round?
A penguin in a revolving door.

What's black and white and has sixteen wheels?
A zebra on roller skates.

What's black and white and white all over?
A scared skunk!

$$\sqrt{\frac{a^2 + \frac{1}{2}b^x}{y^2} \quad \frac{z^3}{a^3} \quad \frac{(a^2 + b^2 + x^2 + y^2)(x^2 - b^3)}{\sqrt{3_x - 2y^3 - z^3}}}$$

What's grey and blue and has a long nose?
An elephant holding its breath.

What is grey and not there?
No elephants.

What is grey and keeps squirting jam at you?
A mouse eating a doughnut.

What is grey, has large ears, a trunk and squeaks?
An elephant wearing new shoes.

What is beautiful, grey and wears glass slippers?
Cinderelephant.

What is grey, has four legs and a trunk?
A mouse going on holiday.

What's grey and lives in the Antarctic?
A melted penguin.

What's grey on the inside and red on the outside?
An inside-out elephant.

What's white and fluffy and lives in the jungle?
A meringue-utan

What is yellow and wears a mask?
The Lone Lemon.

What's big and green and can't fly?
A field.

What's big and red and sits in the corner?
A naughty bus.

What's green and looks like a bucket?
A green bucket.

What's blue and looks like a bucket?
A red bucket in disguise.

What's green and white and bounces?
A spring onion.

What's green and would kill you if it fell out of a tree?
A snooker table.

What's blue and smells like red paint?
Blue paint.

What is green and square?
A lemon in disguise.

What's blue and triangular?
An orange in disguise.

What's long, yellow and fruity?
An apple in disguise.

What's brown and sticky?
A stick.

What's green and flies as fast as a speeding bullet?
Super Bogey!

What's green and jumps a mile without
really meaning to?
A grasshopper with hiccups.

What colour are burps?
Burple.

What colour do cats like best?
Purrrrrr-ple.

What is red and dangerous?
Strawberry and tarantula jelly.

What's orange and sounds like a parrot?
A carrot.

What's pink and fluffy?
Pink fluff.

What's purple and 5,000 miles long?
The grape wall of China.

What's red and bad for your teeth?
A brick.

What's red and green and wears boxing gloves?
A fruit punch.

What's red on the outside, white on the inside and
goes putt-putt-putt-putt?
An outboard radish.

What's yellow and sniffs?
A banana with a cold.

What's yellow and soft and goes
round and round and round?
A long-playing omelette.

What's yellow and stupid?
Thick custard.

What's red and white?
Pink.

Why do elephants wear shoes with corrugated soles?
To give the ants a 50/50 chance.

There is a bungalow in a street. All of the outside of
the house and everything inside the house is painted
purple. What colour are the stairs?
There aren't any stairs. It's a bungalow!

There is a red house on the right and a blue house on
the left. So where would you find the white house?
In Washington DC.

RELIGIOUS STUDIES LESSON

What do you get in December that you don't get in any other month of the year?
The letter 'D'.

How does Moses make his tea?
Hebrews it.

How did Moses part the Red Sea?
He used a sea-saw!

Exam question: What was the name of Noah's wife?
Pupil's answer: Joan of Ark.

What kind of lights did Noah have on the ark?
Flood lights. And ark lights.

Where did Noah keep his bees?
In the ark hives.

Where did Noah keep his fish?
In a multi-storey carp ark.

How does Good King Wenceslas like his pizza?
Deep-pan, crisp and even.

How is it possible to walk on water?
Freeze it first.

Did you hear about the dyslexic Satanist?
He sold his soul to Santa.

The teacher asks, 'What's a Hindu?'
**Marcus puts his hand up and answers,
'It lays eggs.'**

Why did the Buddhist refuse any anaesthetic
when he went to the dentist?
His aim was to transcend dental medication.

A pupil is doing an exam in philosophy.
The exam has just one question on it: 'What is courage?'
'This is!' writes the pupil on his answer paper, signs it, hands it in and walks out.

A religious studies teacher asks the class if they know where God lives.
'Please, miss,' says Anna, 'I think he lives in our bathroom.'
'Why do you think he lives in your bathroom?' asks the teacher.
'Because,' says Anna, 'every morning my dad keeps banging on the door and shouting, "God, are you still in that bathroom?!"'

The religious studies teacher asks the class, 'Who knows where naughty boys and girls go?'
James puts his hand up and says, 'Is it behind the bike sheds, miss?'

One day as part of the religious studies lesson, the class are all taken to church. Afterwards the teacher gets them all to write a letter to God.
Evie writes, 'Dear God, today we all went to church. It was very nice. Wish you could have been there.'

The local vicar comes in to school to meet the children.

When he sees Rosie he says, 'Why hello, Rosie. I heard from your mother that God is sending you a little brother or sister.'

'Yes,' says Rosie. 'And he knows where the money is coming from as well. Or at least that's what I heard Daddy say.'

Jake gets home from school and tells his mum what he learned today in the religious studies lesson.

'Today the teacher kept going on about "ashes to ashes" and "dust to dust",' says Jake. 'What did she mean?'

'Well,' says Mum, 'it probably means that we come from dust and then a long time later when we die we go back to dust.'

A bit later Jake comes running downstairs from his room.

'What's the matter now?' asks Mum.

'I just looked under my bed,' says Jake, looking terrified, 'and either someone has just gone or someone is just coming.'

The religious studies teacher asks Amber, 'What was the name of the first woman?'
'I don't know,' says Amber.
'Think of the first book in the Bible,' says the teacher. 'Do you remember the story about the apple?'
'Oh, I know what her name was,' says Amber. 'Granny Smith!'

The religious studies teacher is reading a passage from the Bible to her class.
'And the Lord appointed a great fish to swallow up Jonah,' she reads, 'and Jonah was in the belly of the fish three days and three nights. Then Jonah prayed to the Lord his God from the belly of the fish, saying, "I called to the Lord out of my distress and He answered me." … and the Lord spoke to the fish, and it vomited out Jonah upon the dry land.'
She puts the Bible down and asks the class, 'Now, children. What do you think this story teaches us?'
'You can't keep a good man down?' says Amelia.

The class is talking about whales. Holly tells the
teacher that she is frightened that if she goes in the
sea, a whale might come and eat her.
The teacher tells her that's not possible. She explains,
'Whales can't really swallow people. Even though
they're really big, they have very narrow throats.
A whale couldn't swallow you even if it wanted to.'
'What about the story of Jonah in the Bible?'
says Holly. 'He was swallowed by a whale.'
'No,' says the teacher. 'That's just a story.'
'No, it's not,' says Holly. 'It's in the Bible. And
when I die I'm going to go to heaven and ask
Jonah how it happened.'
'OK,' says the teacher, 'but what if he's in hell?'
'Then you can ask him,' says Holly.

The religious studies teacher is telling the class about
the Ten Commandments.
She explains the commandment about honouring
thy father and mother and then asks, 'Can any of you
think of a commandment that teaches us how to treat
our brothers and sisters?'
'Yes,' says Nathan. 'Thou shall not kill!'

The religious studies teacher asks Sophie why Joseph and Mary took Jesus with them to Jerusalem.
'Was it because they couldn't get a baby-sitter?' asks Sophie.

The teacher asks the class what name the Israelites called God.
A little girl puts her hand up and says, 'Is it Harold?'
'No,' says the teacher. 'Why do you think they called him Harold?'
'You know,' says the girl. 'Like in the prayer. Our Father, who art in heaven. Harold be thy name...'

SCHOOL PHOTO

The class photograph has just been taken. The teacher tries to encourage the pupils to all buy a copy. 'Just think how nice it will be to look at it when you're older. You can look at the photo and remember all the people you were at school with. You can say, "There's John. Remember how good he was at PE and how he played football every day at playtime? Now he's a famous footballer. There's Alison. Remember how she was always top of the class? Now she reads the news on television." What else do you think you'll say when you look at this picture?'

'There's teacher,' says a voice from the back of the class. 'Remember how she always used to bore us to death? Now she's dead.'

MUSIC LESSON

What has 40 feet and sings?
A choir.

What do you get if you drop a piano on an army base?
A flat major.

What do you get when you throw a piano
down a mine shaft?
A flat miner.

What type of computer keeps singing?
A Dell.

Knock, knock.
Who's there?
Little old lady.
Little old lady who?
I didn't know you could yodel.

How do you turn a duck into a soul singer?
**Put him in the microwave until
his Bill Withers.**

How does Bob Marley like his doughnuts?
With jam in.

What do you call a music teacher with problems?
A trebled man.

What do you call the wife of a hippie?
Mississippi.

What keeps jazz musicians on earth?
Groovity.

What was Jay Z's girlfriend called
before they got married?
Feyoncé.

Why are pianos hard to open?
The keys are inside.

Why are pirates so good at singing?
**They have spent many years working
on the high Cs.**

Why did the music teacher break into song?
He couldn't find the key.

Isaac comes home with two special prize badges from
school – a little badge and a great big badge.
His mum asks him, 'What did you get that little badge
for?'
'For singing,' says Isaac.
'Oh, that's good,' says Mum. 'And what did they give
you the big badge for?'
'For stopping,' says Isaac.

CAREERS ADVICE

What's the difference between a teacher
and a conductor on the railway?
**One trains the mind and the other
minds the train.**

What's the difference between a
butcher and an insomniac?
One weighs a steak and the other stays awake.

What do you call a plumber with a toilet on his head?
Lou.

What do you call a female plumber with
two toilets on her head?
Lulu.

What sort of people decide to become bakers?
Ones who knead the dough.

What do you have to know if you
want to be an auctioneer?
Lots.

What does a tightrope walker have to eat?
A balanced diet.

What do you get if you win 'Dentist of the Year'?
A little plaque.

What do you call a guy who is a lookout
for the Coastguard?
Seymour.

What do you call a teacher with no arms,
no legs and no body?
The head.

What do you call a vicar on a motorbike?
Rev.

What do you call Postman Pat when he retires?

Pat.

What did the Mexican fireman call his twin sons?

Hose A and Hose B.

What do you call the ghost of a
door-to-door salesman?

A dead ringer.

Have you heard the joke about the bin lorry?

It's a load of rubbish.

What has wheels and flies?

A bin lorry.

What's the only school where you have
to drop out to graduate?
Skydiving school.

How many successful jumps does a skydiver
have to do before he graduates?
All of them.

What is the official term for when your
parachute fails to open?
Jumping to a conclusion.

What is the purpose of a propeller on an aeroplane?
**It keeps the pilot cool. And if you
don't believe me, just watch him
sweat when it stops.**

Where do you learn to make banana splits?
In sundae school.

Did you hear about the glass blower who breathed
in when he should have breathed out?
He ended up with a pane in his tummy.

$$\left(\sin\frac{\pi x}{L} - \sin\frac{3\pi x}{L}\right) \quad n = 3 : \omega_2 = \frac{2}{L}\sin^2\frac{3\pi x}{L};$$

What is a chimney sweep's most common ailment?
The flu.

Why don't ambassadors ever get sick?
They have diplomatic immunity.

Did you hear about the optician who fell
into the lens grinder?
He made a complete spectacle of himself!

Have you heard about the garage mechanic who has
become addicted to drinking brake fluid?
He says he can stop any time.

Did you hear about the factory worker who fell into
the upholstery machine?
He's completely recovered now.

Why did the baker stop making doughnuts?
He got sick of the hole business.

Why did the banker lose his job?
He had lost interest.

Why did the car-repair man lose his job?
He didn't, he was just forced to re-tyre.

Why did the computer engineer get the sack?
He had lost his drive.

Why did the woman decide not to become
a hotel receptionist?
She ended up having reservations.

Why did the man get fired from the
car assembly line?
He was caught taking a brake.

Why did the doctor get the sack?
He had completely lost his patients.

Why did the man get sacked from the bakery?
They told him he just wasn't bread for it.

Why did the milkmaid lose her job?
She turned out to be an udder failure.

Why did the other milkmaid lose her job?
She had lost her whey.

Why did the shoe salesman lose his job?
He was given the boot.

Why did the tap dancer retire?
He kept falling in the sink.

Why does a ballerina wear a tutu?
**Because a one-one's too small and
a three-three's too big.**

What is the name for a young army?
The infantry.

Which month do soldiers like least?
The month of March.

What works only when it's fired?
A cannon.

When is the vet busiest?
When it's raining cats and dogs.

Have you heard about the male snake charmer
marrying the female undertaker?
**The towels in their bathroom are marked
'Hiss' and 'Hearse'.**

What do you call a female magician?
Trixie.

What do you call a dead magician?
An abracadaver.

Mr Smith the butcher is 6 feet tall, of average build
and completely bald. What does he weigh?
Meat.

What did the fruit tree say to the farmer?
'Will you stop picking on me?'

Why is getting up for work at five in the
morning like a pig's tail?
It's twirly.

Imagine a bus driver who is travelling down the road.
He goes straight through a stop sign but doesn't slow
down at all. He carries on through a traffic light when
it's on red and goes the wrong way down a one-way
street. Why doesn't he get into any trouble?
**Because he wasn't driving his bus at the time,
he was on foot.**

A man has to call out an electrician and a
plumber to do some work on his house.
One of them turns out to be the father of the
other's son. How could this be possible?
**The electrician and plumber are
husband and wife.**

You're a bus driver. The bus arrives at the first stop and four people get on. At the next stop eight people get on. At the third stop two people get off. At the fourth stop, everyone gets off the bus. Can you tell me what colour the bus driver's eyes are?

They're the same colour as your eyes.
I told you before, you're the bus driver!

Lucas asks his teacher, 'Sir, what's the difference between wages and a salary?'
'Well,' says the teacher, 'if you are paid wages, you get paid every week, but if you receive a salary, you get paid every month. So, for example, I receive a salary and I'm paid every month.'
'Wow! Really?' says Lucas. 'So where do you work?'

Where does success come before work?
In the dictionary.

CHEMISTRY LESSON

Exam question: What is the composition of water?
Pupil's answer: Water is made up of two gins. These are called oxygin and hydrogin. Oxygin is pure gin. Hydrogin is gin plus water.

Exam question: What is the chemical formula for water?
Pupil's answer: H_2O.

Exam question: What is the chemical formula for ice?
Pupil's answer: H_2O cubed.

If H_2O is water what is H_2O_4?
Drinking, bathing, washing, swimming and flushing the toilet.

The chemistry teacher asks Oscar, 'Can you give me
the chemical formula for water?'
'H-I-J-K-L-M-N-O,' says Oscar.
'That's not right,' says the teacher.
'But you told us that,' says Oscar.
'No, I didn't,' says the teacher.
**'Yes, you did,' says Oscar, 'you said water was
"H to O".'**

Exam question: What is water?
Pupil's answer: Melted steam.

How did the chemist hurt herself?
She let the bunsen burner.

Exam question: Name two famous chemists
Pupil's answer: Marie Curie and Boots the.

At the end of the chemistry lesson the teacher
asks his pupils, 'What is the most important thing
that we have learned in the lab today?'
**Max puts his hand up and says, 'Never
lick the spoon.'**

Exam question: What is copper nitrate?
**Pupil's answer: It's overtime pay
for policemen.**

What happens to chemistry teachers when they die?
They barium.

Exam question: What happens to gold
when it is exposed to air?
Pupil's answer: It gets stolen.

The chemistry teacher is showing the class the effects
of different acids. He takes a pound coin and drops it
into a beaker full of acid.
'Now,' says the teacher. 'Does anyone think the pound
coin will dissolve in the acid?'
'No, sir,' says one of the boys.
'Very good,' says the teacher. 'And how do you know
that?'
**'Because,' says the boy, 'if it would, you
wouldn't have put it in there.'**

CAUGHT CHEATING

The teacher says to Rory, 'I hope I didn't see you peeking over at Tom's test paper just then.'
'Yes,' says Rory, 'I hope you didn't see me either.'

The teacher says to Tyler, 'You copied your answers in the exam from Georgia sitting next to you.'
'How did you know that?' asks Tyler.
The teacher says, 'Every time Georgia answered "I don't know" to a question, you've put "Neither do I".'

Dad says to Caleb, 'What did you get in your exam?'
'Zero,' says Caleb.
'Zero!' says dad. 'How did you manage to get zero? Were you off school on the day of the exam?'
'No,' says Caleb. 'But the boy who sits next to me was.'

The teacher has been marking the class's exam papers.

He calls Adam over and says, 'Why have you written "see Edward's paper" next to some of your questions?'

'Well,' says Adam, 'you said we weren't to copy each other's work.'

PALAEONTOLOGY LESSON

Exam question: What is a fossil?
**Pupil's answer: A fossil is an extinct animal.
The older it is, the more extinct it is.**

Why did the dinosaur cross the road?
Because the chicken hadn't been invented yet.

What do you call a very old joke?
Pre-hysterical.

What was the Pleistocene era?
**It was a time when all the dinosaurs were
made from modelling clay.**

What came after the dinosaur?
Its tail.

PALAEONTOLOGY 101

What do you call dinosaurs who suffer
from anxiety attacks?
Nervous Rex.

What do dinosaurs like to put on their pizza?
Tomato-saurus.

What do you call a dinosaur with an
extensive vocabulary?
A thesaurus.

What do you call a blind dinosaur?
Do-ya-think-he-saurus.

What do you call a blind dinosaur's dog?
Do-ya-think-he-saurus Rex.

What do you call a dinosaur who wasn't
able to walk in a straight line?
A staggersaurus.

What do you call the dinosaur who
wrote *Wuthering Heights*?
Emily Brontesaurus.

What weighs 800 pounds and sticks
to the roof of your mouth?
**A peanut butter and
Stegosaurus sandwich!**

Why do you never hear a pteranodon
when it goes to the toilet?
The 'p' is silent.

Which dinosaur is quickest at
wrapping up birthday presents?
A veloci-wrapper.

CITIZENSHIP LESSON

Have you heard about the recent survey?
**Apparently six out of seven dwarfs said
they weren't happy.**

Why do socialists drink herbal tea?
Because they believe proper tea is theft.

The teacher asks the class, 'Does anyone know
the name of the Speaker of the House?'
'Yes,' says Sophia, 'it's Mummy.'

Knock, knock.
Who's there?
Justice.
Justice who?
Justice once, let me in please.

What did the bald man say when he was
given a comb for his birthday?
'Thank you! I shall never part with it.'

$$\frac{x^2 - y^2}{\sqrt{z^2}} = 2\sqrt{\frac{(x - y^2)(3z + 2r - y^2)}{a^2 + b^2}}$$

What do you call a girl who has to be
helped around a lot?
Carrie.

What do you call a girl who is extremely conceited?
Mimi.

What do you call a man who lives in a back street?
Ali.

What goes: 'Boo hoo hoo hoo splat splat'?
Someone crying their eyes out.

What goes: 'Ha ha ha ha plop'?
Someone laughing their head off.

What is the definition of being born to succeed?
A budgie with a blunt beak.

Where does Friday come before Monday?
In the dictionary.

How do you keep an idiot in suspense?
I'll tell you next week.

PE LESSON

What does PT stand for?
Physical Torture.

What do you call a man with a load of sports equipment on his head?
Jim.

Letter received excusing a pupil from the PE lesson:
'My son is under a doctor's care and should not take PE. Please could you execute him today.'

What does the winner lose in a race?
His breath.

In which lesson do you learn how to run through all the countries of the world?
Jog-raphy.

How did the barber win the race?
He knew a short cut.

Why was the football pitch so wet?
Because the players kept dribbling over it.

What do you call a girl who stands
between two goal posts?
Annette.

A teacher starts work at a new school in north
London.
She says, 'I support Arsenal. Does anyone else
support Arsenal?'
All the children put their hands up apart from Amy.
The teacher asks her who she supports and she says
'Tottenham Hotspur.'
'OK,' says the teacher, 'so why do you support them?'
**'Because my dad supports them and so does
my mum and my brother.'**
'OK,' says the teacher. 'But you don't have to be the
same as the rest of your family. What if your dad was
an idiot and your mum was an idiot and your brother
was an idiot? What would that make you?'
**'Well, then,' says Amy, 'I suppose it would
make me an Arsenal supporter.'**

One boy says to another, 'I bet you a pound I can predict the score of any game of football before it begins.'
'Go on then,' says the friend. 'Predict the score of the match this afternoon before it begins.'
'OK,' says the boy. 'Nil-nil. That's always the score before a game begins.'

Mum is telling one of her friends that her little boy has been chosen to be in the school cricket team.
'That's good,' says her friend. 'What position are they putting him in?'
'I'm not sure,' says Mum. 'I think they said he was going to be one of the drawbacks.'

What can you catch but not throw?
A cold.

What can you make disappear just by standing up?
Your lap.

What do you get if you cross an overweight golfer and a pair of very tight trousers?
A hole in one.

What's the difference between a bad golfer and a bad skydiver?
One goes 'Whack. Oh no!'
The other goes, 'Oh no! Whack.'

Who can hold up a bus with one hand?
A lollipop lady.

The PE teacher asks Hugo, 'Why are you swimming on your back?'
'Because I've just had dinner,' says Hugo, 'and you told us we shouldn't swim on a full stomach.'

Why are you not supposed to swim on a full stomach?
It's easier to do it in a swimming pool.

A schoolboy goes to the swimming pool where he climbs to the highest diving board.

He is just lifting his arms and is ready to dive when his teacher comes running out of the changing rooms and says, 'What are you doing? There's no water in the pool today!'

'That's alright, sir,' says the boy. 'I can't swim.'

Letter received excusing a pupil from the PE lesson:
Please excuse Matthew from PE for a few days. Yesterday he fell out of a tree and now he has misplaced his hip.

Knock, knock.
Who's there?
Dwayne.
Dwayne who?
Dwayne the swimming pool quickly, I'm dwowning!

DESIGN AND
TECHNOLOGY LESSON

Exam question: What is a turbine?
**Pupil's answer: It is something Monty Panesar
wears on his head.**

How do you get frogs to do DIY?
Give them some toadstools.

What do you call a woman with a screwdriver in one
hand, a knife in the other, a pair of scissors between
the toes on her left foot, and a corkscrew between the
toes on her right foot?
A Swiss Army wife.

How do you make anti-freeze?
Hide her nightie.

Knock, knock.
Who's there?
Cargo.
Cargo who?
Car go beep beep.

What do you call a man with a car on his head?
Jack.

What kind of car does Humpty Dumpty drive?
A Yolkswagon.

What's got four wheels, runs on petrol and whizzes around in a French cathedral?
The Hatchback of Notre Dame.

When is a car not a car?
When it turns into a driveway.

Knock, knock.
Who's there?
Isabel.
Isabel who?
Isabel necessary on a bicycle?

What award do they give the designer of door knocker of the year?
The No Bell Prize.

What has four legs but never stands?
A chair.

What has four legs but only one foot?
A bed.

When is a door not a door?
When it's ajar.

What did the first lift say to the second lift?
'I feel like I'm coming down with something.'

Have you heard the joke about the roof?
Don't worry, it's way over your head.

HORTICULTURE LESSON

What do you call something that runs round your
garden all day and night and never stops?
A fence.

What goes hoe, hoe, hoe?
Father Christmas doing his garden.

What is the difference between one yard
and two yards?
A fence.

Have you heard the one about the two
snowmen standing in a field?
**One turns to the other and says, 'Do you smell
carrots?'**

What do you call a girl who's got caught in a fence?
Barb.

What do you call a man who has a spade on his head?
Doug.

What do call a man who has recently had
a spade taken off his head?
Douglas.

What do you get hanging from cherry trees?
Sore arms.

What's brown and sits on the wall?
Humpty's dump.

CHILDREN AT SCHOOL
CAN BE SO CRUEL

A boy runs home from school crying.

'Mummy,' he sobs. 'All the boys at school call me big head.'

'That's terrible, son,' says Mum. 'It's so unkind and it's just not true. Now go to the shops and get me three pounds of apples, five cabbages and a bag of potatoes.'

'OK,' says the boy. 'But how can I carry all that lot back?'

'Just do what you usually do,' says Mum. 'Stick them in your balaclava.'

A little boy arrives home from school one day with tears running down his face.

'Oh dear. What's the matter?' asks his mum.

'The other children at school all laughed at me in the playground,' says the little boy. 'And they kept saying I looked like a werewolf.'

'That's ridiculous,' says his mum. 'They were just silly, cruel, nasty little children.'

'So I don't really look like a werewolf, Mummy?' asks the little boy.

'No, of course not,' says his mum. 'Now dinner's nearly ready so why don't you go and dry your eyes and give your face a comb.'

KERB DRILL

Why did the chicken cross the road?
To get to the other side.

Why did the chicken cross the road?
How should I know? Ask the chicken!

What do you call a chicken crossing the road?
Poultry in motion.

What would you have if Batman and Robin
were run over by a bus?
Flatman and Ribbon.

Why did the hedgehog cross the road?
To visit his flat mate.

Why did the chicken stop in the middle of the road?
She wanted it to lay it right on the line.

Why did the duck cross the road?
It was the chicken's day off.

Why did the cow cross the road?
To get to the other side.

Why did the sheep cross the road?
To get to the other side.

Why did the turkey cross the road?
He wanted to prove he wasn't chicken.

Why did the farmer cross the road?
To go and get all his animals back.

LATE AGAIN

Dear Teacher, this is to let you know that Wendy will
be absent from school tomorrow as we have to attend
her funeral.

Jasper sets off to school walking very slowly.
'Hurry up! You'll be late!' his mother shouts after him.
**'It's alright,' says Jasper. 'They're open till
three-thirty.'**

The teacher tells Ryan, 'You're late! You should have
been here at nine o'clock.'
'Why?' says Ryan. 'What happened?'

Jack says to his dad, 'I can't go to school today. I don't
feel very well.'
'Oh dear,' says dad. 'Where don't you feel well?'
'In school,' says Jack.

The school secretary answers the phone and hears a voice say, 'Hello. I'm afraid Henry won't be able to come into school today.'

'Oh dear,' says the secretary. 'Who's that speaking?'

'This is my father,' says the voice.

The teacher asks Freddy, 'Why were you late?'

'Sorry, sir,' says Freddy. 'I overslept.'

'I can't believe it,' says the teacher. 'You mean you have to sleep at home as well?'

The teacher asks Stephen, 'Why are you late for school?'

'Sorry, miss,' says Stephen, 'I was dreaming of a football match.'

'Why did that make you late?' asks the teacher.

'It went into extra time,' says Stephen.

Did you hear about the boy who was late for school?

He'd seen a sign up the road that said 'School – go slow'.

Did you hear about the student who played truant
from his correspondence school?
He kept sending them back empty envelopes.

Dear Teacher, I'm sorry Danny wasn't able to come to
school yesterday. He was suffering from diarrhoea and
his boots leak.

The teacher says to Zoe, 'Did you miss school
yesterday?'
'Yes,' says Zoe, 'but not very much.'

Why was the elephant late getting on the plane?
Because he had forgotten his trunk!

Dear Teacher, Please excuse Hannah for missing
school yesterday. We forgot to get the Sunday paper
out of the mail box and when we found it on Monday,
we thought it was Sunday.

A dad says to his son, 'I heard that you didn't bother going into school today and went and played football all day instead.'

'That's not true at all,' says the boy, 'and I've got the fish to prove it.'

The teacher tells Charlie, 'This letter from your dad excusing you from school yesterday looks like it was written by you.'

'Yes it does, doesn't it?' says Charlie. 'It's probably because he borrowed my pen to write it.'

MARINE BIOLOGY LESSON

Exam question: Where do you find the world's largest mammals and why?
Pupil's answer: The world's largest mammals are found in the sea. This is because there is nowhere else to put them.

Why did the dolphin cross the beach?
To get to the other tide.

What lies at the bottom of the sea and shivers?
A nervous wreck.

What goes cruising down the riverbed at 60 miles an hour?
A motorpike with two side carps.

What is an eel's favourite dance?
The conger.

What TV game show do fish like best?
Name that tuna.

What type of fish can't swim?
Dead fish.

What did the beach say when the tide came in?
'Long time, no sea.'

What did the fish say when it swam into a wall?
Dam.

Where do you find the most fish?
Between the head and the tail.

Why did the crab go to jail?
Because it had been caught pinching.

Which outlaw lives at the bottom of the sea?
Billy the Squid.

What lies at the bottom of the sea and
terrorises the other fish?
Jack the Kipper.

What's 12 feet long, has big teeth,
goes up and down and eats people?
A shark in a lift.

Where do you go to find out the weight of a whale?
The whale-weigh station.

Why did the fish blush?
He had just seen the boat's bottom.

Why didn't the lobster share his toys?
He was a bit shellfish.

What do you find in the middle of a jellyfish?
Its jellybutton.

What do you get if you cross an octopus with a cow?
An animal that can milk itself.

What did the boy octopus say to the girl octopus?
'I want to hold your hand, hand, hand, hand, hand, hand, hand and hand.'

What do you call a man with no arms and no legs who has fallen in the sea?
Bob.

What do you call a woman who's good at catching fish?
Annette.

What do you call a woman with a boat on her head?
Maude.

What do you call an octopus with no tentacles?
Puss.

What do you call a guy who puts his right hand into the mouth of a giant white shark?
Lefty.

What do you get if you cross a fish with an elephant?
Swimming trunks.

Did you hear about the red ship that collided with a blue ship?
All the survivors were marooned.

Imagine you are in a sinking rowboat surrounded by sharks. How would you survive?
Well, one way would be to just stop imagining it.

What's the best place to go shopping on the ocean?
The harbour. There are sails everywhere.

Where do ships go when they're not well?
To the docks.

Three men are in a boat. The boat capsizes but only two of the men get out of the water with their hair wet. How did the third one get away with it?
He was bald.

What do you get if you cross the Atlantic Ocean with the Titanic?
About halfway.

PETS' CORNER

What has four legs, claws, whiskers and a tail, and can see equally well from both ends?
A blind cat.

What kind of dog can jump higher than a building?
Any kind of dog. Buildings can't jump.

What looks like a dog, eats dog food, lives in a kennel and is extremely dangerous?
A dog with a machine gun.

What's a dog's favourite subject at school?
Dog-raphy.

What's invisible and smells like rabbits?
Rabbit farts.

What's the most difficult thing about milking a gerbil?
Getting the bucket underneath it.

When is a black dog most likely to
come into your house?
When you leave the door open.

Where do you find a one-legged dog?
Exactly where you left it.

What does a cat say when he overtakes you at 100
miles an hour on the motorway?
'Meeeeeeaaaaaaaooooooouuuuuuwwww.'

What does a dog become after it is six years old?
Seven years old.

What do you get if you cross Lassie with a pit bull?
**A dog that bites your leg off and then
runs to fetch help.**

What do you get if you cross a parrot with a shark?
A bird that will talk your ear off.

What do you get if you cross a pit bull with a chicken?
Just the pit bull.

What do you get if you cross a hairy dog
with a telephone?
A Golden Receiver.

What do you get if you cross a dog with a giraffe?
**An animal that keeps barking at
low-flying aircraft.**

What do you get if you cross a dog and a lion?
A petrified postman.

What do you get if you cross a dog with a frog?
**A dog that can lick you from the other
side of the road.**

What do you get if you cross a cat with a gorilla?
An animal that puts you out at night.

What do you get if you cross a cat with Godzilla?
A town remarkably free of dogs.

What do you get if you cross a cat with a canary?
Shredded tweet!

What do you call a rabbit with fleas?
Bugs Bunny.

What do you call a cross between a cocker spaniel,
a poodle and a cockerel?
A cocka-poodle-doo!

Where do dogs park their cars?
In a barking lot.

What do you call a cross between a lemon and a cat?
A sour puss.

Did you hear about the dog who went
to the flea circus?
He stole the show.

Daisy takes her dog on a 'take your pet to school' day.
There were going to be prizes for the best behaved,
cutest and cleverest pets.

Daisy is determined her dog will win a prize and gets
him to perform a whole series of tricks. The judges
are impressed but still not sure.

**'Will you give him the prize if he can answer a
maths problem?' asks Daisy.**

The judges agree so Daisy turns to the dog and asks,
'How much is two plus two minus four?' The dog
does absolutely nothing.

**Daisy turns back to the judges and says,
'Right, so can I have my prize now please?'**

GEOGRAPHY LESSON

The geography teacher tells Kayla, 'You didn't get anything right in your geography test. What's your excuse?'

'Well,' says Kayla, 'my dad says the world is changing every day so I didn't think there was much use revising until things have settled down a bit more.'

The geography teacher asks Leo, 'Can you tell me how you would prove the world is round?'

'No,' says Leo. 'And besides, I never said it was.'

The geography teacher unrolls a map of the world and asks who knows where America is.

George puts his hand up and the teacher beckons him to the front of the class where he indicates America on the map.

'Well done, George,' says the teacher and then turns to the rest of the class. 'Now who knows who discovered America?'

'George did!' say the rest of the class.

How did the geography student drown?
His grades were below C level.

What do you call a guy who likes reading maps?
Miles.

Why are mountains so funny?
Because they're hill areas.

What is the definition of a volcano?
A mountain with hiccups.

What has a bed but does not sleep and a mouth
but does not speak?
A river.

Why are rivers always rich?
Because they have two banks.

Why don't people ever steal canals?
There's too many locks on them.

Why was the seabed wet?
Because the sea weed.

Where is the ocean deepest?
At the bottom.

Where can you find an ocean with no water?
On a map.

Exam question: Explain what causes ocean tides.
**Pupil's answer: The tides are caught up
in a fight going on between the earth and
the moon. As we all know, nature abhors a
vacuum and because there is no atmosphere
or water on the moon, the water on the earth
all gets sucked towards it. During the day the
moon disappears so things settle down for a bit.**

The teacher asks, 'Can you define what an island is?'
**Samuel answers, 'An island is an area of land
which is completely surrounded by water apart
from one side.'**
'What do you mean?' asks the teacher. 'Apart from
which side?'
'The top side,' says Samuel.

The geography teacher asks Millie, 'Where's the English Channel?'
'I don't know,' says Millie. 'We can't get it on our television.'

The geography teacher asks, 'How would you describe the rain in this part of the country?'
'Like little drops of water that keep falling from the sky,' says Martha.

Why is Britain such a wet country?
Because the queen has been reigning there for years!

What's the best way to stop water coming into your house?
Don't pay the water bill.

Ten people are all sheltering beneath a small umbrella and yet none of them gets at all wet. How do they manage it?
It was not raining at the time.

What's worse than raining cats and dogs?
Hailing taxis.

What did the first meteorologist say to the second meteorologist?
I'm feeling a bit under the weather today.

Why do meteorologists look worried?
Their future is always up in the air.

Why does lightning shock people?
Because it doesn't know how to conduct itself.

What kind of pants do clouds wear?
Thunderwear.

What do you call a guy who gets struck by lightning?
Rod.

What type of rocks do you never find in the ocean?
Dry ones.

What happens when you drop a green
stone into the Red Sea?
It gets wet.

What do you call a man with a boulder on his head?
Squashed.

Exam question: Explain how dew is formed?
**Pupil's answer: The sun shines down on the
leaves and makes them perspire.**

Exam question: Explain one of the processes by which
water can be made safe to drink.
**Pupil's answer: Water can be made safe to
drink by the process of flirtation which helps
remove large pollutants like grit, sand, dead
sheep and canoeists.**

Have you heard the joke about the three deep holes
drilled in the ground?
Well, well, well.

What is the difference between the
North Pole and the South Pole?
All the difference in the world.

What do you call a chicken at the North Pole?
Lost.

What do Eskimos get from sitting on the ice too long?
Polaroids.

What do you call an igloo that doesn't have a toilet?
An ig.

Why are igloos round?
To stop penguins hiding in the corners.

Why don't polar bears eat penguins?
They can't get the wrappers off.

What lives at the Arctic and looks unhappy?
A bi-polar bear.

What do you call a snowman with a suntan?
A puddle.

What do you sing at a snowman's birthday party?
Freeze a jolly good fellow.

The teacher asks Zachary, 'Can you name an animal
that lives in Lapland?'
'Yes,' says Zachary. 'A reindeer.'
'Very good,' says the teacher. 'But can you name
another?'
'Yes,' says Zachary. 'Another reindeer.'

Exam question: Where is Felixstowe?
Pupil's answer: It is on the end of Felix's foot.

If Ireland sank into the sea which
county would stay afloat?
Cork.

How do you make a Venetian blind?
Poke him in the eye.

Knock, knock.
Who's there?
Europe.
Europe who?
No I'm not, but you are.

What is bamboo?
It's the sound made by an exploding ghost.

What city has the largest rodent population?
Hamsterdam.

What do you call a French man in sandals?
Philippe Philoppe.

What do you call an Irishman with rice
growing in his garden?
Paddy.

What do you call an Irishman who looks
forward to the summer?
Paddy O'Furniture.

What do you call a Spaniard who can't find his car?
Carlos.

What do you call a Spanish man with a rubber toe?
Roberto.

What lies in the middle of nowhere?
The letter 'H'.

What travels round the world always
staying in the same spot?
A stamp.

Where do dogs live?
Bark-shire.

Whereabouts in the world do they
make all the films about parrots?
Pollywood.

Which place in China is famous
for its car horn factory?
Hong King.

Dad asks his son if he enjoyed the school geography
trip.
**'Yes I did,' says the boy, 'but we've got to go
back again tomorrow.'**
'Why's that?' asks Dad.
**'We've got to try and find the kids that got left
behind today,' says the boy.**

PERSONAL, SOCIAL AND
HEALTH LESSON

The teacher asks Arthur, 'Can you complete this
famous quotation? "Cleanliness is next to..."'
'Impossible,' says Arthur.

What do you call a fairy that doesn't
like to have a bath?
Stinkerbell.

How do you keep your hair dry in the shower?
Don't switch the water on.

What's white when it's dirty and
black when it's clean?
The school blackboard.

How do you make a tissue dance?
You just put a little boogie in it.

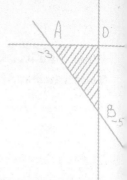

Knock, knock.
Who's there?
Anita.
Anita who?
Anita tissue ... ah-choo!
Too late!

Knock, knock.
Who's there?
Atch.
Atch who?
Bless you. Do you need a tissue as well?

What is the only effective cure for dandruff?
Baldness.

What should you buy if your hair keeps falling out?
A good vacuum cleaner.

How can you get a set of teeth inserted free?
Wind up your dog.

What time is it when it's time to go to the dentist?
Tooth hurty.

What did Godzilla eat after having
his teeth fixed by his dentist?
His dentist.

What should you do when your nose goes on strike?
Picket.

What did the hat say to the scarf?
You hang around while I go on ahead.

How do you make a cigarette lighter?
Take out some of the tobacco.

If Mr and Mrs Bigger have a baby, which of them
would be the biggest?
The baby. Because he's a little Bigger.

Judy was born on 31 December and yet she always
celebrates her birthday during the summer. Why?
She lives in Australia.

What grows up while growing down?
A goose.

Oscar's mother had three children. The first child
was named April. The second child was named May.
What was the third child's name?
Oscar.

Exam question: Describe what happens to a person's
body as they age?
**Pupil's answer: When you get old, so
do your bowels, and eventually you get
intercontinental.**

Can a man marry the sister of his widow?
No. He's dead. That's why his wife is a widow.

A woman shoots her husband, then holds him
underwater for five minutes and finally, she hangs
him. A few minutes later, they both go for dinner
together. How is this possible?
The woman is a photographer.

A man is condemned to death. He is told he must choose to walk into one of three different rooms. In the first room there is a fiery inferno. In the second room are 100 deadly assassins with loaded guns ready to shoot him. And in the third room there are a pack of lions who haven't eaten for three months. Which room should he choose?

The third room: if the lions really hadn't eaten in three months they would all be dead.

Is it legal for a man living in Scotland to be buried in England?

No it isn't. It's never legal to bury people who are still alive.

A man is entirely dressed in black. He has a black suit, black shoes and a large black hat. He walks down a street where all the street lamps are off. A black car, with its headlights switched off, speeds down the road but comes to an emergency stop before it hits the man. How did the driver manage to see him in time?

It all happened in the daytime.

Did you hear about the man who got
too big for his breeches?
He was exposed in the end.

Have you heard the joke about the pavement?
It's all over town.

If a girl falls down a well why can't her
brother help her out?
**Because he can't be a brother and
assist her as well.**

Knock, knock.
Who's there?
Matthew.
Matthew who?
Matthew lathe hath come undone.

$$\left(\sin\frac{\pi x}{L} - \sin\frac{3\pi x}{L}\right) \; n=3 \cdot \omega_2 = \frac{2}{L}\sin^2\frac{3\pi x}{L};$$

Knock, knock.
Who's there?
Woo.
Woo who?
OK, there's no need to get so excited.
It's only a joke.

What do you call a man with no arms and
no legs sitting on your front porch?
Matt.

What do you call a girl who has one leg
shorter than the other?
Eileen.

Why did the one-handed man cross the road?
To get to the second-hand shop.

Why did the leper crash his car?
He had left his foot on the accelerator.

Why did the leper go back into the shower?
He had forgotten his Head and Shoulders.

What do you call a guy who can't light firecrackers?
Dud.

What do you call a man wearing a raincoat?
Mac.

What do you call a man wearing two raincoats?
Max.

What do you call a man with a pole
going through his leg?
Rodney.

What do you call an accident-prone driver?
Rex.

What do you call someone who keeps talking
when no one is listening?
A teacher.

What do you do if you find a sick bird?
Give it first-aid tweetment.

What do you give the man who has everything?
Antibiotics.

What do you take off last before you get into bed?
Your feet off the floor.

What does a person with two left feet wear?
Flip-flips.

What's a royal pardon?
It's what the queen says after she burps.

What's the definition of a will?
Come on, you must know.
It's a dead giveaway!

What's the difference between an oral thermometer
and a rectal thermometer?
The taste.

When does New Year come before Christmas?
Every year!

When is it unlucky to see a black cat?
When you are a mouse.

Why are there so many Smiths in the phone book?
They all have phones.

Why did the tooth spend all day making
itself look nice?
**It had heard that the dentist
was taking it out later.**

Why doesn't Santa allow his little helpers
to drink beer?
Because it's bad for your elf.

What did Jack the Ripper's mum keep saying to him?
**'No wonder you're still single, you never go
out with the same girl twice.'**

What did the stupid burglar do when he saw
a 'Wanted' poster with his face on?
**He phoned up the police station to
apply for the job.**

What do you call a boy called David after he
becomes a victim of ID theft?
Dav.

A class from school is being shown round the local
police station. The officer shows them pictures of the
ten most wanted criminals in the local area.
One of the boys asks if these are genuine pictures of
genuine criminals.
'Yes,' says the policeman, 'of course they are.'
**'So why didn't you just arrest them all when
you were taking their pictures?' says the boy.**

Exam question: Name a major disease
associated with cigarettes.
Pupil's answer: Premature death.

Is it true that an apple a day keeps the doctor away?
Yes, if you aim it right.

The teacher notices a boy giving a big yawn in the class.

'Remember your manners,' says the teacher. 'When you yawn, you should put your hand over your mouth!'

'I can't do that,' says the boy. 'I'd get bitten.'

The teacher tells David, 'You've got your shoes on the wrong feet.'

'What do you mean?' says David. 'These are the only feet I've got.'

EXCUSED TO GO
TO THE TOILET

The teacher notices that one of the girls in her class has a puddle under her seat.
'You should have put your hand up,' says the teacher.
'I did,' says the little girl. 'But it trickled through my fingers.'

If you're an American in the kitchen,
what are you in the bathroom?
European.

Charlie asks the teacher, 'Can I go to the toilet?'
'OK,' says the teacher, 'but only if you can recite the alphabet.'
'OK,' says Charlie. 'A-B-C-D-E-F-G-H-I-J-K-L-M-N-O-Q-R-S-T-U-V-W-X-Y-Z.'
'That was quite good,' says the teacher, 'but what happened to the "P"?'
'Right now,' says Charlie, 'it's going halfway down my leg.'

Knock, knock.
Who's there?
Eye dunap.
Eye dunap who?
**Poo-ee, I thought you had.
Couldn't you have waited till
you got to the toilet?**

PHYSICS LESSON

Why did the chicken cross the Möbius strip?
To get to the same side.

Exam question: Define 'momentum'.
**Pupil's answer: A momentum is what you give
a person when they are going away.**

The science teacher asks, 'Who can give me the name
of a liquid that won't freeze?'
'I can, miss,' says George. 'Hot water.'

Which weighs more, a ton of feathers
or a ton of bricks?
Neither – they both weigh a ton!

Exam question: Give an example that demonstrates
that light travels faster than sound.
**Pupil's answer: A person who appears bright
until you hear them speak.**

Which is faster – hot or cold?
Hot. You can catch a cold.

How do you start a fire with two sticks?
Make sure one of them is a match!

Imagine you only have one match. You enter a dark
room in which you find an oil lamp, some newspaper
and some kindling wood. Which would you light first?
The match.

Exam question: What does Boyle's law state?
Pupil's answer: A watched kettle never boils.

Exam question: What had Archimedes discovered
when he leaped out of the bath and shouted 'Eureka'?
**Pupil's answer: A big spider near the plug
hole.**

Which burns longer, the candles on a girl's birthday
cake or the candles on a boy's birthday cake?
Neither. They both burn shorter.

Why was the candle excited all day?
He was going out that night.

What can turn without moving?
Milk.

What does a clock do when it's hungry?
It goes back four seconds.

Does a match box?
No, but a tin can!

What goes down but never goes up?
An elephant in an elevator.

What goes up and down but doesn't move?
A staircase.

What goes up white and comes down yellow and white?
An egg.

Two atoms are walking down the street.
One says to the other, 'I think I just lost an electron.'
'Are you sure?' asks his friend.
'Yes,' says the first, 'I'm positive.'

Did you hear about the school science teacher who handed out dead batteries?
They were free of charge.

The science teacher asks Amy to explain why the law of gravity is useful.
'Well,' says Amy, 'the law of gravity is important because if we drop something, it's much easier to get it from off the floor than off the ceiling.'

Have you read the book about anti-gravity?
I just couldn't put it down.

Why is the sky so high?
So birds don't bump their heads.

Exam question: What is a planet?
Pupil's answer: A planet is a body of earth surrounded by sky.

The teacher asks the class, 'What's a comet?'
'A star with a tail,' answers Florence.
'Very good,' says the teacher. 'And can anyone name a star with a tail?'
'Yes,' says Rory. 'Mickey Mouse.'

What does the USS *Enterprise* and toilet paper have in common?
They both circle Uranus looking for black holes and trying to wipe out the Klingons.

What's the difference between a Martian and a potfer?
What's a potfer?
It's a thing you use to cook your dinner in, dumbo!

What's the difference between a Martian and snoo?
What's snoo?
Nothing much. What's snoo with you?

WOODWORK LESSON

A teacher goes up to a boy working away in the woodwork class.

'What are you making?' she asks.

'It's a portable,' replies the child.

'Oh yes,' says the teacher. 'A portable what?'

'I'm not sure,' says the boy. 'So far I've only made the handle.'

Jonathan gets home from school and tells his dad,

'The woodwork teacher doesn't like the things I keep making.'

'Oh dear,' says dad. 'What sort of things do you keep making?'

'Mistakes,' says Jonathan.

Have you heard about the wooden car with the wooden wheels and the wooden engine?

It wooden go.

What can you put into a box that will make it lighter?

Holes.

What do you call a man with a lump
of wood on his head?
Edward.

What do you call a man with two lumps
of wood on his head?
Edward Wood.

What do you call a man with three lumps
of wood on his head?
Edward Woodward.

What do you call a man with four lumps
of wood on his head?
I don't know but Edward Woodward would.

Why does Edward Woodward have so
many D's in his name?
**Because if he didn't, he'd be called
Ewar Woowar.**

ZOO VISIT

How do you get down off an elephant?
You don't, you get down off a duck.

How do you stop an elephant from charging?
Take away his credit card.

How does an elephant hide in the jungle?
**He paints his toenails red and sits
in a cherry tree.**

How do you get an elephant to sit in a cherry tree?
**Plant a seed, let the elephant
stand on it and wait.**

What did Tarzan say when he saw a herd of elephants
coming over the hill?
**'Look, a herd of elephants coming
over the hill!'**

What did Tarzan say when he saw a herd of elephants
with sunglasses coming over the hill?
Nothing. He didn't recognise them.

How hard is it to spot a leopard?
**You don't have to bother because
they come that way.**

What did the buffalo say to his son
when he left for college?
'Bye, son.'

What did the idiot call his pet zebra?
Spot.

What do giraffes have that no other animal has?
Baby giraffes.

What do you get if you cross a bear with a skunk?
Winnie the Phew.

What do you call a camel with a flat back?
Humphrey.

What do you call a flying hippo?
Dangerous.

What do you call a bear whose hair is falling out?
Fred bear.

What do you get if you cross a giraffe with a cockerel?
An animal that can wake up people living on the top floor.

What do you get if you cross a kangaroo and a sheep?
A woolly jumper!

What do you get if you cross a kangaroo
with an elephant?
Enormous holes all over Australia.

What do you get if you cross an elephant
with a parrot?
**An animal that tells you absolutely
everything it remembers.**

What do you get if you cross an elk
with a cocoa bean?
Chocolate moose.

What do you get when an elephant blows its nose?
Out of the way.

What do you get when an elephant skydives?
An extremely large hole.

What does an elk wear if it doesn't
want to be recognised?
A false moosetache.

What has two grey legs and two brown legs?
An elephant with diarrhoea.

What has two humps and is found at the North Pole?
A lost camel.

What has two tails, two trunks and five feet?
An elephant with spare parts.

What is a zebra?
It's 25 sizes larger than an 'A' bra.

What is as big as an elephant and the same shape as an elephant but weighs absolutely nothing?
An elephant's shadow.

What kind of monkey is able to fly?
A hot-air baboon.

What should you do if you find an elephant in your bed?
Find somewhere else to sleep.

What time is it when an elephant sits on your fence?
Time to buy a new fence.

What would you call a friend who
has an elephant on his head?
Your flat mate.

What's the best way to catch a gorilla?
Hide in a tree and make a noise like a banana.

What's the difference between an elephant
and a flea?
**An elephant can have fleas but a flea can't
have elephants.**

What's the difference between an elephant's
bottom and a letter box?
**Well, if you don't know, I'm not going
to ask you to post my letters.**

Which side of a penguin has most feathers?
The outside.

Why can't penguins fly?
They're not tall enough to be pilots.

Why are elephants all wrinkly?
You've obviously never tried to iron one.

Why are lions slow to apologise?
It takes them a long time to swallow their pride.

Why did the parrot wear a raincoat?
So he would be polyunsaturated.

Why do elephants have big ears?
Because Noddy won't pay the ransom.

Why do elephants never forget?
Nobody ever tells them anything.

Why do flamingos lift up one leg?
Because if they lifted up both legs they'd fall over.

Why do giraffes have such long necks?
Because they have such smelly feet.

Why do gorillas have big nostrils?
Because they have big fingers.

Why do we have reindeer?
To water the grass, darling.

Why is an elephant big, grey and wrinkly?
Because, if it was small, white and smooth it would be an aspirin.

HOMEWORK

Alfie says, 'Dad, I'm tired of doing my homework.'
'Now, son,' says Dad, 'I've told you before, hard work
has never killed anyone.'
**'I know,' says Alfie, 'but I still don't want to
risk being the first one.'**

Dad gets home and finds little Johnny in the front
room, sitting on a horse and writing something in his
school exercise book.
'What's going on?' asks Dad.
**'Well,' says Johnny. 'The teacher told us that
for our homework we had to write an essay
on our favourite animal. So that's why I'm
here and Sally's sitting in the goldfish bowl.'**

Rhys hands in his homework and the teacher is
amazed.
'This is the first homework you've handed in this
month,' says the teacher, 'what's happened?'
**'Oh nothing,' says Rhys, 'it's just this time I
was busy last night so I didn't have time to
think up a good excuse.'**

The English teacher is looking at Anna's homework. 'One of your essays is very good,' says the teacher, 'but I can't read the other one. What's going on?'
'Sorry, sir,' says Anna, 'but my mum's handwriting is much better than my dad's.'

The English teacher says to Millie, 'For your homework, one of the questions was to spell the word "tomorrow" but you have spelled the word "today" instead.'
'I know,' says Millie. 'That's because I did my homework yesterday.'

Freddie goes to ask his friend Joseph if he can come out to play.
'Sorry,' says Joseph. 'My dad's told me I've got to stay in tonight and help him do my homework.'

Dad asks George, 'How are you getting on with your history homework?'

'Really good,' says George. 'The teacher told us we could use the Internet to research the answers.'

'Any good?' asks Dad.

'Yes,' says George. 'So far I've found five places that are selling them.'

Henry asks his dad, 'Dad, could you do my homework for me?'

'No,' says Dad. 'It wouldn't be right at all.'

'I know it wouldn't,' says Henry, 'but at least you could have a go.'

Ollie calls to his dad: 'Dad, I've got maths homework tonight. Can you help me find the lowest common denominator?'

'Oh!' says Dad, 'they made me look for that when I was at school. Don't tell me they still haven't found it yet.'

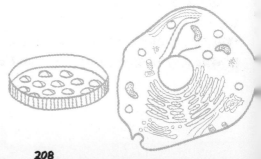

The English teacher asks Tom to read out the story he has written for his homework.

Tom reads, 'Athgy grhaw djow glgp fgtbo wflkygh stryu haxzc blblblblbxxz.'

'That's absolute rubbish,' says the teacher.

'I know,' says Tom. 'But you told us we had to do it using our own words.'

The teacher asks Orla, 'Did your parents help you with your homework?'

'No,' says Orla, 'I got it wrong all by myself.'

The teacher is looking at Francesca's homework and tells her, 'Your spelling is much better. Only five mistakes this time.'

'Oh good,' says Francesca.

'Right,' says the teacher, 'now let's have a look at the next word.'

The teacher is reading Jack's homework.

'Your handwriting is absolutely terrible,' says the teacher.

'Yes,' says Jack. 'But look on the bright side. If it was any better you'd realise I can't spell.'

The teacher says to Jake, 'This homework you've written about your dog is exactly the same as the one your sister wrote for me last year.'
'Well, yes, it would be,' says Jake. 'It's the same dog.'

The teacher calls James over and says, 'Tell me the truth now. Your father helped you do this homework, didn't he?'
'No, he didn't,' says James. 'He did it all on his own.'

EXAMS AND RESULTS

Dad asks Ryan, 'So, did you pass all your exams?
'No,' says Ryan. 'But on the plus side, I came top of all the people who failed.'

Dad is looking through Nathan's report.
'This is terrible,' says Dad. 'It says that you've come bottom in a class of 20.'
'Look on the bright side, Dad,' says Nathan. 'It could have been worse if there had been more people in the class.'

Dad says to Elliott, 'Can I see your report, son?'
'Sorry,' says Elliott. 'My friend borrowed it to scare his mum and dad.'

Jack comes home from school and says, 'Mum, can you write with your eyes closed?'
'Yes, I think so,' says Mum. 'Why do you ask?'
'I need you to sign my school report,' says Jack.

Amber comes home from school and tells her dad,
'I've failed every exam except for algebra.'
'Oh well, that's something,' says Dad. 'So how did
you manage to avoid failing that?'
'I didn't take it,' says Amber.

Zac says to his teacher, 'I don't think I deserve a zero
for this homework.'
**'Neither do I,' says the teacher, 'but it's the
lowest mark I can give you.'**

Did you hear about the boy who was the school swot?
**The other children used to pick him up and
use him to wallop flies with.**

What's the best way to get a pat on the head?
Sit beneath a cow.

Have you heard about the pupil who was so dumb he
had to have 'left' and 'right' written on his feet so he
would know which way round to put his shoes on?
**If he'd been able to read he would
have been fine.**

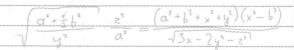

Jasmine has to do an exam paper comprising a series of questions all with 'yes' or 'no' answers. She spends the first half of the exam continually tossing a coin and filling in the answers accordingly. If she tosses heads, she marks an answer 'yes', if it's tails she marks it 'no'.

She quickly finishes the exam and then spends the rest of the time re-reading the paper and tossing the coin over and over again.

'What are you doing?' asks the teacher.

'It's alright, sir,' says Jasmine. 'I'm just going through the paper again checking my answers.'

Daniel asks his teacher, 'Is it right to punish someone for something they haven't done?'

'No, of course not,' says the teacher.

'Good,' says Daniel, because I haven't done my homework.'

Sophie's mum asks her, 'Why are your exam marks so poor this year?'

'It's all the teacher's fault,' says Sophie.

'But,' says Mum, 'you've got the same teacher as you had last year and your results were OK then.'

'I know,' says Sophie, 'but last year I was sitting next to Chloe who's really brainy, and now the teacher's moved her.'

The invisible boy's mother asks, 'Why have you got such bad marks on your report?'

'Because the teacher keeps marking me absent,' says the invisible boy.

The teacher asks Callum, 'How do you manage to get so many things wrong in a day?'

'I get up early,' says Callum.

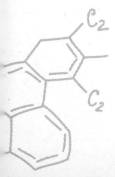

THE PARENT-TEACHER MEETING

Aidan comes home and tells his dad, 'We've got to go to a small meeting of the Parent Teacher Association tomorrow.'

'A small meeting of the Parent Teacher Association?' says Dad, surprised. 'How many are going to be there?'

'Just you, me and my teacher,' says Aidan.

Dad goes in to meet his son's teacher.

'What do you think my son will be when he finishes school?' asks Dad.

'Quite an old man,' says the teacher.

It's parents' evening and Jason's teacher looks over his exam papers and tells his dad, 'Well, there's one positive thing I can say about Jason's performance.'

'Oh good,' says Dad. 'What's that?'

'With results this bad,' says the teacher, 'he can't possibly have been cheating.'

Mum and Dad are concerned about their son Oscar's progress at school so they go in to see his teacher. 'Oscar wasn't doing very well at first,' says the teacher, 'but I've given him a few hours' extra tuition and now he's getting straight As.'
'That's fantastic,' say his parents.
'Yes,' says the teacher, 'now we just have to move on to the rest of the alphabet.'

Have you heard about the little boy whose mum and dad had to go into school so often, they ended up with a better attendance record than he had?

Dad asks his son, 'How do you like going to school?'
'Well, says the son, 'I don't mind the going bit, and the coming-home bit is OK. It's just the bit in between I'm not keen on.'

Dad asks his son, 'How do you like school?'
'Closed,' says the son.

Dad gets home from parents' evening and he is furious. 'What's going on, son?' asks Dad. 'Your teacher has just told me that he finds it impossible to teach you anything!'
'See,' says the boy. 'Didn't I tell you he was useless?'

Isabelle comes home from school and tells her mum, 'I think we need a new teacher at school.'
'Why is that?' asks Mum.
'The one we've got doesn't know anything,' says Isabelle. 'She keeps asking us for the answers all the time.'

William comes home from school and tells his mum,
'Today the teacher asked me if I had any brothers or sisters.'
'Oh really?' says Mum. 'And what did she say when she found out you were an only child?'
'She looked up to heaven with a big smile on her face and said, "Thank God for that!"' says William.

If teachers are so smart, then why are they in school?

If teachers are so smart, why are they the only ones who have to have a book with the answers in it?

Why did the cross-eyed teacher get the sack?
Because she was unable to control her pupils.

Who were the invisible man's mum and dad?
His transparents.

Ruby and Evie are talking about their new primary school teacher.
'How old do you think she is?' asks Ruby.
'I don't know,' says Evie. 'But she looks quite old.'
'We could look inside her knickers and find out,' says Ruby.
'How is that going to tell us how old she is?' asks Evie.
'It'll have it written inside,' says Ruby. 'In mine it says, "six to seven years".'

The teacher tells the class, 'We're only going to have half a day of school this morning.'

'Hooray!' say the class.

'We'll have the other half this afternoon,' continues the teacher.

Two little girls are talking about their teachers.

'Our teacher keeps talking to herself during the lesson and she doesn't seem to realise it at all,' says one little girl.

'So does our teacher,' says her friend. 'I'm beginning to wonder if she might think we're listening to her.'

It's the end of summer term at primary school and the children bring presents for their teacher.

The son of the local florist presents the teacher with a well-wrapped cone.

'I bet I can guess what this is,' says the teacher, giving the package a shake and sniffing at it. 'Is it flowers?'

'Yes it is,' says the boy.

The next child to bring her a present is the daughter of the local sweetshop owner. The teacher takes the present from her and gives it a little shake.

'Mmmm,' says the teacher. 'Is it chocolates?'

'Yes it is,' says the girl.

Finally, the son of the local off-licence owner comes up with his present. The teacher takes the box from him, shakes it and notices a trickle of amber liquid coming from one corner.

She tastes a drop and asks, 'Is it a box of wine?'

'No,' says the boy, 'it's a puppy.'

THE SCHOOL PRAYER AT THE END OF THE LAST DAY BEFORE THE END OF TERM

One more day of school,
One more day of sorrow,
One more day of this old dump,
And I'll be home tomorrow!

This edition published in the United Kingdom in 2015 by
Portico
1 Gower Street
London
WC1E 6HD

An imprint of Pavilion Books Company Ltd
Copyright © Pavilion Books Company Ltd 2015

ISBN 978-1-91023-201-9

A CIP catalogue record for this book is available from the
British Library.

10 9 8 7 6 5 4 3 2

Reproduction by Mission Productions Ltd, Hong Kong
Printed and bound by Bookwell, Finland

This book can be ordered direct from the publisher at
www.pavilionbooks.com